FAREWELL TO EMPIRE

A BROWN SAHIB STORY

BY DAVID DATTA

Typeset by Tanglewood

The front cover shows Dr. Datta in his 1927 Bull Nosed Morris

Printed in Times Roman by
Clarke Printing, Monmouth

To the Grandparents I never met.

Prologue

Austin and I met up in the Old Tavern to plan our journey to Oxford the following week. It would be my first day at Wadham College. He had already completed a year at Brasenose and made his mark by becoming librarian, and playing Rugby and Water Polo for the College. My accident would preclude any sporting activities and after two years in uniform I felt decidedly apprehensive about whatever academic demands might lie ahead. The only consolation I could find was that at least I had sat and passed the entrance exam and thus proved to myself that I was not merely relying for my place on the personal friendship between my ex-headmaster, John Garrett, and the Warden, Maurice Bowra.

It was likely that we would travel by coach. We had too much luggage for my motor-cycle and I felt disinclined to ask my father to drive us. He would gladly have done so, being immensely proud of having a son at Oxford, but I felt I had made too many demands on his paternal devotion in recent years. He would have gone to the ends of the earth for either of his sons, and in my case he had done precisely that.

We sipped our George's draught bitter, and Austin gave me pointers about what to expect. He was well involved in his studies and equally proud of some of the decidedly classy characters he had met there. As a pianist he was hugely impressed by meeting someone whose godfather was the great Moiseiwitch, and almost equally so by a man called Walters, whose family made all the nation's toffee.

'You'll spend the first year in college,' he explained, 'then move into digs, which is much cheaper. Maybe we can fix something up together in due course.'

There were one or two familiar faces in the pub, and then 'Inky' arrived. We nodded a greeting but kept our distance. 'Inky' was my neighbour. He lived in a fine Victorian villa which had a small factory attached, in which the family had produced 'Taylor's Gravy Browning'. His name was Gerald and his nickname derived from the fact that they also made ink, which most people believed to be the same concoction under different labels. 'Inky' was an alcoholic. Once a tall, handsome fellow, the demon drink had made him a sad figure to be laughed at and avoided. After a couple of months production he would close his factory down and go on a prolonged bender. It looked as though he might be starting one that very evening. He was harmless enough, but he owned a Rolls Royce Phantom, vintage 1930, which he would insist on driving when in his cups, his licence having been revoked many times over. His main jeu d'esprit was to telephone the local police station and inform the duty sergeant whenever he planned to take to the road.

It was a little before closing time when he sidled up to us.

'Nice to see good friends relaxing,' he slurred. 'I've heard all about your exploits, David,' he said. 'Tell me, what are you doing these days?' I explained that I was due to go up to Oxford next week, and my friend was already there.

'Oxford indeed,' said Gerald. 'What a lovely place.'

Then a thought struck him. 'How are you getting to Oxford?' he asked. I mentioned the coach.

'My dear young gentlemen,' he said. 'Coaches are not for you. Look, I have to go to Oxford next week on business. I should be delighted to drive you there.' If I had doubts about the offer, I suppressed them. The thought of saving two fares was not easily dismissed.

We thanked him warmly, and agreed to be at his house on the morning scheduled.

The idea of arriving at Oxford on my first day in a Rolls Royce, had a certain cachet. Neither Zuleika Dobson nor the Bridesheads could have done it better.

***

When the day came we climbed aboard, in Royal style. My mother offered a silent prayer for our survival and waved us goodbye from the bottom of the drive. I gave her a gracious twirl of the hand from the passenger seat and we rumbled off up the road to Gloucester.

Gerald, at the wheel, seemed perfectly competent and we relaxed to the manner born, amid the polished walnut and soft leather.

We left the city behind us, and came to Almondsbury. Gerald took his foot off the accelerator and the car slewed into the forecourt of the first pub on the open road.

'One for the road, boys,' he said cheerfully.

Austin and I exchanged apprehensive glances but we followed in to the bar. Gerald ordered a double scotch and downed it with a pint of bitter. We each drank a half of shandy. As a true alcoholic, the merest taste of the stuff wrought an immediate change in Gerald. Up to that point he had been perfectly normal, if perhaps a little tense. Now his movements became erratic, his speech decidedly slurred. Austin reminded him that we had a long way to go. Somewhat reluctantly he led the way back to the car. Behind him, Austin grabbed my shoulder and hissed, 'You've got to get at the wheel of that car. Otherwise we're never going to make it.'

I took his cue. 'Gerald,' I said, 'I've never driven a Rolls Royce. Do you think I might have a go?' 'Certainly, dear boy,' he said, and handed me the key. I clambered aboard, studied the antiquated instruments and managed to distinguish the gear lever from the hand brake, both of which were on the right hand side.

'Double de-clutch on all gears,' said Gerald helpfully. I felt like a passenger being asked to steer an ocean liner. Once under way I managed to get it into top and we headed for Gloucester. At such a date there were almost as many farm carts as cars on the road, and I made it past them with loud blasts from the klaxon, at speeds of anything up to twenty m.p.h.

The size and solidity of the vehicle gave confidence. I could manage the gears reasonably well, but on the road I kept the flickering speedometer well below the forty mark. Soon another pub appeared on the left, and I felt Gerald shift in his seat.

'Drives beautifully,' I said to occupy his mind.

'A Rolls is a Rolls' agreed Gerald.

I sensed that the main hazards on the road were not the hay carts or herds of cows, but the regular occurrence of inviting hostelries. I had to pretend not to notice them. We managed twenty miles or so of stately progress, and then I realised that Gerald was less than happy about my cruising speed. Occasionally a faster vehicle overtook us, and this led to a decided twitching. He also began to gaze with added interest at any approaching pub. I worked out the necessary equation. In order to keep Gerald out of the pubs, I would have to drive much much faster; pride of ownership demanded it. A twenty year old Rolls Royce Phantom with a lunar mileage on the clock is no vehicle for rally drivers. At over 50 m.p.h. a decided shudder ran through its venerable frame, and at 60 this became an all pervading shake.

But I had no choice. Gerald was only happy if he was the fastest car on the old A38. The process meant hair-raising overtaking with arrogantly un-British blasts on the horn for the good of all concerned. Farm carts, grocer's vans, Daimlers, Morrises and Lanchesters all rapidly gave way, and Gerald beamed proudly. After a nerve wracking hour, I piloted the car to a halt outside the ancient New Inn at Gloucester, and we tottered inside for a legitimate and necessary liquid lunch.

The road over the Cotswolds produced a new hazard. There was no way that I would allow Gerald to take the wheel again now that he had reached a state of alcoholic stasis. This meant driving at speeds as high as the car could manage. At nearly seventy it shook from end to end, but kept direction like a thoroughbred. Then a new kind of drama arose With much sounding of horns and hand signalling, I was in process of overtaking an Austin Seven on a road with a far distant bend. The needle flickered past seventy, and then to my horror the engine went dead. We were stranded on the wrong side of the road with a truck coming towards us. Then, seemingly seconds from disaster, the engine took up again, and we got safely through. I heard Austin call his saviour's name from the back seat.

'Ah, she does that occasionally,' muttered Gerald. 'Don't know why. Sometimes I put a drop of my own stuff in the tank and she misfires.' The 'stuff' was obviously a chemical used in his factory. What made the process worse was the occasional presence on the road of huge U.S. Army Rio trucks bearing down on us with complete contempt for all native road users. There were several of these as we fought our way through Witney, then Burford, and by the time we reached Oxford I felt I was shaking quite independently of the car. But we reached the dreaming spires, and I slewed to a halt in the High Street. Austin scrambled out and heaved the suitcases onto the pavement.

Our departure was far from gracious. Muttering thanks we left Gerald looking somewhat lost and alone. Perhaps his business meeting was a pure fiction, and he had merely needed company. We said hasty goodbyes, leaving him to cope in the way that he was well used to, avoiding accidents, arrest and even German bombs in the Blitz.

In those days, it seemed, Heaven smiled indulgently on Rolls Royce drivers even when far gone in their cups.

Chapter 1

In the Summer of 1937 every British schoolchild was presented with a mug filled with chocolates to celebrate the Coronation of King George VI. His nervous countenance gleamed from the gift, alongside that of his Queen, formerly Elizabeth Bowes-Lyon.

An inscription recorded the importance of the occasion and there were ample symbols of Royalty and Imperial majesty in red white and blue.

To a nine year old the edible contents were highly acceptable. The rest was merely a confirmation of what we all knew in the deep heart's core. That we were British, that we belonged to the greatest nation on earth, and that the British Empire was the greatest the world had ever known. Our exercise books carried a projection on the back cover showing a world dominated by British possessions, clearly shown in pink. Yes, America was very big and Russia too covered a large expanse; but if you took in all the pink areas including Canada, much of Africa, India and the enormous span of Australia, there was no contest. Britain was biggest and best. Every year in May, most schools celebrated "Empire Day" for which teachers were supposed to give special lessons on the good things we were doing all over the World, and there were regular Empire exhibitions at which one could buy brassware from the Punjab or carved crocodiles from Africa.

And all this vastness was owned and controlled by two little blobs at the top that were the British Isles.

The contrast simply provided proof, if it were needed, of the superiority of the Island Race and a few chocolates, with a picture of the new King, were a tasty confirmation of the fact.

In my case the school was a typical Church of England Primary school in Fishponds, Bristol, called Dr. Bell's after a much respected religious educationalist. My father was himself a doctor, in charge of a mental hospital. He could have afforded to send me to a local Prep school but he had reasons for giving me a grounding in real life. Socialism was one motive, and the ability to take the rough and tumble amid the sons of pottery and engineering workers were also good notions. For all that it was an excellent school; the three "r"s were dinned in properly, and the headmaster, a wonderful chap called Cook, was devoted to Bristol's maritime past and taught us all the great sea shanties, remembered to this day with lines like "...throw him in the scuppers with a hosepipe on him!"

Religion was of course de rigeur but Cookey managed to give our Christianity a Kiplingesque bias with hymns like "Onward Christian Soldiers" that somehow fitted the pink on the backs of our exercise books and the faces on our Jubilee mugs.

In those days of nicotine innocence, the grown-ups all smoked and we collected their cigarette cards. My favourite collection was 'Ships of the Royal Navy', and one could look proudly at these mighty expressions of Imperial Naval power; with their swivelling gun turrets and huge 15 or 16 inch guns, these mighty craft seemed fit to dominate the world's oceans. HMS Hood, Renown, Rodney, Warspite and so many others were the envy of all other nations, and when they held a review, the most envious people of all were the recently defeated Germans. Only years later when these great ships lay on the bottom did we learn what our confident superiority would lead to.

Being middle class in a state primary school meant that one's father was almost unique in owning a motor car; in which he took us on wonderfully adventurous holidays (like the Betjemans) in Cornwall, or truly foreign places like Yorkshire and even the three day journey to Scotland where my mother was shocked to see barefoot children.

Most children if they were lucky enough to have holidays, settled for a couple of happy days riding donkeys at Weston-Super-Mare, a short train ride away.

But there came one incident that caused class consciousness to create an unforgettable mental implosion. We were told to ask our mothers for proper P.T. kit on sports days: a white vest, blue shorts and black daps. 'Daps' was the Bristolian argot for Plimsolls (odd that, since the great benefactor Plimsoll was himself a local man.)

The teacher inspected us all in our kit and then stopped in horror at a boy who was wearing white tennis shoes. He had him out in front of the class and tore into him for his disobedience.

'Why, boy, do you dare to wear white shoes when I told you black!' he raged. The nine year old drew himself proudly up and looked the teacher in the eye. 'Sir,' he said, 'my mother said she cannot afford to buy me new shoes for P.T. I have to make do with her old ones which are white.' The simple logic destroyed the teacher's sarcasm. The boy wore his white shoes on all sports days, and won many events.

He was a boy I would see much of over the years that followed. I was probably alone in enjoying the irony of his later action when he was a director of a merchant bank that bought the shoe factory, a local manufacturer of Plimsolls, and closed it down. In no way a vindictive action, but motivated purely by Stock Market considerations. However I anticipate events.

Social life in the thirties did not forever focus on great class differences. Car ownership made a difference, but foreign travel was a rarity even for the comparatively well off. Those who had to count their pennies carefully, led very similar lives to those who bought suits made to measure. In a prosperous town like Bristol, all classes seemed able to watch the Rovers play, or witness the great Wally Hammond hitting sixes. There were sports clubs for all who needed them, and far more satisfaction to be got from digging your allotment, than from to-day's celebrity obsessed Television. The young had their Youth Hostels and Ramblers' Association, Ballroom dancing had a huge following, tennis clubs flourished. The horrors of the First World War were far behind us, the slump and the general strike had become distant memories, the idea of a second World War seemed like a Wellsian absurdity.

We revelled in British achievements; in the building of the great liners like the Queen Mary, which could outpace the French Normandie, and which so impressed the Americans they couldn't believe they hadn't built it themselves.

While the Japanese still rode in rickshaws, we made the best cars in the world, like Rovers, Daimlers, Lanchesters, Austins and Morrises, and if you visited London, the Rolls Royces seemed bumper to bumper. Although there were pockets of poverty made manifest by unemployment among South Wales miners or in the slums of the North, few could deny the huge economic advantages that flowed into Britain from its vast Empire. The very rich, whose mansions and estates owed much to earlier centuries of slave owning, and nouveau riche Mill and foundry entrepreneurs, were able to expand in number in a way unknown on the Continent. For the Middle Classes, there were huge employment opportunities; everyone knew someone who had gone to plant tea in India, or tap rubber in Malaya. The best brains, if they failed to make it into the Foreign Office, could become respected civil servants in India or the colonies. If you felt like a career in the Services, there were plenty of "dissident" tribes to bomb in Iraq, or Afghanistan.Teachers who favoured travel could make for Church schools in Nigeria or the West Indies. A great merchant fleet employed thousands building ships, or sailing them to far flung outposts. The great expansion of semi-detached suburbia, owed much to this activity.

And there was plenty of cheap food for those gainfully employed, with Canadian wheat, New Zealand lamb, South African fruit, and for me there were above all Jamaican bananas. I hit on a recipe of mashed bananas and cream which became an addiction. It fortified me for my six mile bicycle ride to school, restored me on my return to listen to Conan Doyle's "Lost World" on the Wireless, and guaranteed peaceful slumbers at night. In Bristol the banana boats came right into the city centre. Dozens of men with barrows sold them at a penny each all over town. Life without bananas became unthinkable.

And how did a Doctor, who had come here from India in 1911 and married an Englishwoman fit into this relaxed world? To every observer he would have seemed to be utterly at home, in accepting English mores, and to lead a life of calm domestic satisfaction.

In fact, however, he had an intellectual life too that took him into the realms of historical necessity and dialectical change, a life quite unknown to the people who surround us. He read books by a man called Karl Marx, he followed the career of V.I. Lenin, and as a doctor dealing with the mentally inadequate he carefully considered the speculations of Sigmund Freud, Jung, Adler, Kretschmer and others. All books that were firmly closed to the rest of his family, and to a developing seedling like myself. For he had an almost religious dedication to the sanctity of the family, and never an ounce of mental pressure was brought to bear on any of us.

Only occasionally did unconventional interests throw light on his inner thoughts. In 1938 he stayed up into the small hours of the morning, listening on short wave radio to a broadcast from America. I too heard part of it as the strange voice faded or boomed against a background of atmospherics that sounded like Atlantic Rollers. One caught phrases like "straight left" and "right uppercut". The

"What spires, what farms are these?"

The author's painting of Snowdon House where he was born and lived for 22 years. The seventeenth century house stood at the top of Snowdon Road, Fishponds, Bristol. It was demolished by Bristol City Council in 1959. The shire horse was called Captain.

matter that had won his attention was nothing less than the World Heavyweight Boxing Championship, the return match between the champion Max Schmeling of Germany and Joe Louis, the black American whom he had previously deposed. In fact the fight did not last long. In the very first round Louis, the Brown Bomber, put Schmeling on the canvas several times, then ended the matter with a knockout punch. Shufflin Joe had conquered the man Adolf Hitler regarded as a living symbol of the supremacy of the German race. The descendant of a slave had become a hero of black and white Americans alike.

My father's satisfaction can only be imagined. But it was not something he made much of among colleagues and family. Such occasions were an entirely private satisfaction. In every other respect he was the devoted father of a British family; playing tennis at his club, driving us out to picnics in the Mendips or the Cotswolds. Out of friendship for another doctor colleague, an entirely non political warmly creative man called Lucas, he was even persuaded to become a Freemason.

Personal relationships were never to be infringed.

And nothing more exemplified the principle than Christmas. One might have expected the grandson of an orthodox Hindu, with leanings towards dialectical materialism, to be somewhat cool about the festive season.

Instead, ours were the most dedicated Christmas imaginable. Decorations, lavish presents (a Hornby train or a new bicycle for me) culminated in the approved Turkey roast with home made puddings and pies to make a scene worthy of Dingly Dell. The conventional gluttony was usually shared with the family of my brother's fiancée which helped to add a certain properly patriotic note. Old man Brain had served in the army in India, but suffered no racialist hangovers, and he had three pretty daughters to guide through life so if one of them married the son of an Indian doctor the social cachet absolutely eliminated any negative thoughts caused by his army life out East.

But his presence did ensure a proper observance of the essentially Imperial quality of Christmas. At 2p.m. all chatter ceased, cutlery was put aside, and the radiogram was turned up loud so that we could all listen respectfully to the manful efforts of George V1 to address the nation as he struggled with a speech impediment which no-one was so disrespectful as to notice.

The high emotional focus of the whole event was such as to compel even my father to lay aside any thoughts of the October Revolution, labour conflicts in America, or the progress of Messrs Gandhi, Nehru and the Congress party of India, and to listen humbly to the King Emperor as he spoke to the obedient millions of all hues in all corners of the globe. Such occasions were greatly fostered by the house in which I was fortunate enough to have been born. Snowdon House was a stone built edifice which had begun life perhaps 400 years before, as a farmer's dwelling, set in sixty acres. Its walls were of three foot thick stone, and there were still built-in settles, and evidence of inglenook fireplaces beneath rough hewn oak beams. The house and its grounds did not belong to us but I grew up feeling it was entirely my principality and even my inheritance. By such illusions could one combat the very occasional slights directed from uncouth locals at a boy with a brown skin. They were infrequent; but they registered, and one learned to deal with them without undue pain.

After all, I lived in a darn sight bigger house than yours, chum.

Only once did a shaft strike home. We were on holiday, Betjeman style, at Newlyn in Cornwall. One evening after dinner my father and I went for a stroll along the quayside. Two small boys were playing there and on seeing us they were seized with mirth. "A blackie! A blackie!" they shouted, capering about in childish disbelief. My father always carried a silver topped walking stick, and I called on him to use it on the little savages.

'Oh no, one must never do that,' he said simply. It was my first lesson in survival.

I went to Bristol Grammar School in 1937 and there was joined by Austin Davis. The difference was my dad paid the nine pounds a term; but Austin won a scholarship. Nor would it be the last time he did so. But we made the school Rugby team together and formed a sporting bond that seemed capable of withstanding every other pressure.

Within the two years that followed even callow youths became aware of the worries German national behaviour was causing. But it was still a marginal matter. If we thought about the Germans at all it was to admire their health and strength philosophy with much hiking and camping. My brother even hummed a German song. "Bei mir bist du schoen..." totally unaware of any significant connotations in the fact that it was a Jewish song.

Of course the Germans didn't want war. As kids we revelled in conflict of an entirely different kind. Every local cinema like the Vandyke, Fishponds, offered what became known as the 'fourpenny rush'. Crowds of excited kids, the boys all wearing holsters with toy six shooters, packed in to watch Tom Mix and his brave pioneers, forming their covered wagons into circles while the dastardly Indians whooped and galloped around them firing bows and arrows and even Winchesters. The audience screamed with rapture as the Indians bit the dust. Heroes tugged arrows from their shoulders and fired volley after volley from their Colt 45's. The audience noise was so intense that the manager often came on stage and threatened to stop the show unless order was restored.

Week after week we had all the violence we craved. We were Tom Mix, Buck Rogers, Gene Autry, in turn, and we fought off rustlers as well as Indians. None of your John Ford, John Wayne, Gary Cooper sophistication here. We knew the only good Indian was a dead one. Every time a cowboy pulled a trigger, five Indians fell from their horses; thanks to brilliant shooting, plus the fact that Indian extras were paid ten dollars a day more for pitching out of the saddle and biting the dust.

We could all draw our six-guns in a flash of silver, we could fan the hammer and above all we could roll over and die, twisting and turning as we expired; cursing and gurgling, and sometimes even staggering to our feet again to loose off one last shot, and let our opponent try and perform his death scene just as convincingly.

But cinema did not totally replace Gutenberg. In between

wrestling with our stuffy school literature, we filled our testerone spawning world with "Comics". Square jawed heroes like Rockfist Rogan could fight there way out of trouble in magazines like Adventure, Wizard, Hotspur. They were the tough guys who had displaced the more genteel inhabitants of the Magnet, like Billy Bunter, or those in the more proper organs of Empire like the Boy's Own Paper.

In all this it gave a thrill sent from Heaven above when I heard that Tom Mix himself was to visit England and would perform his great riding and shooting act at the Bristol Hippodrome. Naturally I begged my father to take us. Understandably he was reluctant. How could I know what he knew too well; that the first great genocide of the nineteenth century was carried about the European immigrants on the native peoples of North America, and Tom Mix epitomised the whole race of horse mounted killers that had carried it out. But such was the family devotion of my father that he took me to see Tom Mix. On can only guess in retrospect at the lip-biting moments he experienced as the man in the tall stetson rode his magnificent white horse onto the stage, and blasted away at his targets with pearl handled Colts, and shotguns. I thrilled at the sight and sound of it.

How little did I know that there would soon be far bigger bangs all over the City of Bristol and Cowboys and all they stood for would become a celluloid irrelevance.

And there was even worse to come.

There would be no more bananas.

Chapter 2

In 1920 my father's brother Ullaskar was released from prison after twelve years of penal servitude, having originally been sentenced to death.

The occasion was an amnesty granted to all political prisoners by King George V at the end of the Great War.

In 1909 the province of Bengal had been in turmoil thanks to a plan by the great Lord Curzon ("My name is George Nathaniel Curzon. I am a most superior person") to partition it and link much of the Eastern side with Assam. My uncle had taken part in a plot to assassinate a certain magistrate, Mr. Kingsford, who had a reputation for handing out savage sentences to those involved in the Independence movement. He had helped to make a bomb which a man called Ghosh had thrown at Kingsford's carriage. The only occupants had been two English ladies who were both killed.

Questions had been asked in Parliament about the death sentence, and this was eventually commuted to life imprisonment. He was sent to the Andaman Islands, the British equivalent of the French Devil's Island. In Britain many have heard of the latter, but few know about the former. The local crop was mustard, and penal servitude meant working a treadmill in temperatures of up to 100 degrees F. He was also given periods of solitary confinement. After twelve years his sanity had become questionable and he wrote a book about prison life in which many incidents of fantasy occur, including a meeting with Queen Mary.

The whole affair had been quite devastating for my grandfather and his family. His forbears in West Bengal belonged to an ancient Hindu tradition quite distinct from that of the Moslems of East Bengal, who would ultimately become a separate nation. West Bengal had always had high cultural standards, producing reformers like Ram Mohan Roy, poets like Tagore, and even early film makers. They kept in touch with European thinkers like Voltaire, Rousseau, Mill and English literature from Shakespeare to Dickens. My grandfather had a certain reputation as a member of the Brahmo Somaj group which was concerned to extract and popularise the most progressive ideas embodied in the Sanskrit texts, the Vedas. At the age of twenty he had gained a high reputation for delivering a series of lectures on the concepts of spirit and material existence. His approach was strongly monistic and anti-dualism, and he found the doctrines of the Christian Trinity quite preposterous. Many Christians secretly agree. He published several books, and his work found favour with the English Theosophical movement of Annie Besant, and the Sanskrit researches of the German Professor Max Mueller.

Then in 1885 he became convinced that what India needed was not more philosophy but modern agriculture. He won a scholarship to the recently founded Royal Agricultural College at Cirencester, where his name still adorns the honours board in gilt letters.

On his return to Bengal he bought several hundred acres of hill country and began to do battle with snakes and tigers. One tiger attacked a local peasant and my father aged fifteen went bravely forth armed with an ancient muzzle loader. Perhaps fortunately for him, the farmer pointed to his broken spade. The tiger had attacked his cow, his most vital means of subsistence, and the peasant had counter attacked, putting the tiger to flight. Unfortunately the syllabus at Cirencester had not covered such eventualities.

In due course my grandfather became Principal of Sibpore College, and a deputy Magistrate. He published two books "Peasant Proprietorship in India" and "Landlordism in India" which became standard works of reference for generations of students. There was no question of his complicity in the Kingsford affair, but with one son facing the hangman's noose a shadow fell over the whole family. Another son was a research chemist in the U.S.A., and it was from him that Ullaskar derived his knowledge of explosives. In those days there was no Internet to give instructions. He was not charged, but the promise of a government job never materialised.

Although my father was still in his teens, they were all under such surveillance that his mother pleaded with him to go away, and

ironically the safest place for him to be was England
He arrived in London in 1909.

My uncle and his collaborators, called the "Jugantar" were naturally dubbed "terrorists". Only an anti-colonialist would question the language used in such situations. But if Winston Churchill had considered plans to assassinate Adolf Hitler he would hardly have been called a "terrorist". When the Czech underground murdered the Nazi S.S. Chief Heydrich, they were called "freedom fighters"; but when the Germans wiped out the town of Lidice in reprisal, it was they who were the terrorists. Even the C.I.A., thinking up ways to remove Castro, were not strictly terrorists; simply would be assassins. Clearly terrorists kill the innocent as well as the guilty. The I.R.A. and Al Quaeda espouse terrorism. My uncle did not.

When my father arrived in London he found a room in Red Lion court, and enrolled at the London Tutorial College. His eventual aim was to read for the bar. Then came two meetings which were to change his whole life, The first of these was in the form of a handsome young man who befriended him, called David Garnett. He was studying zoology, a course which had previously been taught by no less than H.G.Wells. For a lively but unsophisticated young man from India the meeting proved to be Exodus and Revelations rolled into one. He was taken to the very apex of European Arts and Literature. Garnett's father Edward was fluent in several European and classical languages, and became a librarian at the British Museum, a post which brought him into contact with virtually every literary celebrity from Shaw to Virginia Woolf and from Rupert Brooke to J.M.Keynes. His mother Constance met Tolstoy and became renowned as the translator of Dostoevsky, Gogol, and Tchekhov into English. David grew up as a close friend of John Galsworthy, Ford Madox Ford and D.H.Lawrence. When Ford founded "The English Review" he met a whole host of literary luminaries like Henry James; it was a coterie so all encompassing that it is faintly absurd to refer to them as "Bloomsberries". My father retold with pleasure the moment witnessed by his friend, when Constance went

into Edward's office with a whole sheaf of manuscripts and said;
'I think you ought to take a look at this my dear. It's by a Polish chap who writes remarkably good English. He calls himself "Conrad."' It was indeed a heady introduction to English life and letters for someone who had previously only known a British person as a member of an occupying power and would be expected to address him, if at all, as "Sahib". At college his charisma soon won David Garnett's devotion and he invited him to stay at his parents' house, The Cearne, in Surrey. Inevitably the matter of Ullaskar's imprisonment was aired and Garnett was soon drawn into sympathy with the Indian Independence movement. His parents' involvement with Russia and the anti- Czarist movement there gave him a natural bond with anti-colonialist thinking. But he found my father resolutely against continued violence. In his autobiography he quoted him verbatim;

"Killing an honest honourable man who is doing his best; killing him because of a general situation for which he is in no way responsible, cannot be right."

In a short space of time Garnett however was quite seduced by the Indian activists he met through my father and in due course he became involved in activities that could easily have landed him in prison. Politically conscious Indians in London tended to gravitate towards a remarkable man called Sarvakar, and all of them were constantly under police surveillance, especially since there had been an attempt to assassinate Curzon. The Garnetts were much involved in the foundation of an artistic colony at Letchworth Garden City, itself a famous example of future town planning. One day my father decided to go there. Letchworth lay ten miles or so beyond the tram terminus, and my father decided to walk it. Ten miles on foot was no great distance for a Bengali, but after while on country roads he became aware that there were two men plodding behind him. It was a hot day in high Summer. After an hour or so, one of the men caught up with him and said, with a pained expression;
'Mr. Datta, do you propose to walk much further?'

My father turned on a mixture of surprise and pleasure and replied;

'Only to Letchworth, sir. But it is a long way isn't it. Would you gentlemen care to join me for a cup of tea?' They found a nearby tea shop and settled down for a long and amicable chat.

"Counter espionage English style" my father called it.

During the months that followed, an odd juxtaposition took place between Garnett and his Indian friend.

My father had become totally enamoured of the London theatrical scene. He went to see many of the great names of the day, including Harley Granville Barker and Beerbohm Tree, (something he was to remind me of, a little scornfully when in later years I tried to persuade him to come and see Olivier's "Hamlet"). He also became utterly entranced by Italian opera and Verdi in particular. Meanwhile Garnett had become mesmerised by the Indian Independence movement to which my father had introduced him. He then embarked on a course of action which could easily have led to his own incarceration.

The most dynamic Indian leader in London was Sarvarkar, who had already persuaded a follower to try and assassinate Lord Curzon himself. Sadly, there was yet another case of mistaken identity and the man he shot was Curzon Wylie, a British civil servant who was largely sympathetic to Indian aspirations. For this and other activities, Sarvarkar was held on remand in Brixton prison, and Garnett conceived an extraordinary plan to help him escape. After his own experiences my father wanted no part in this, but he came up with a suggestion that he and a friend would go to Morocco and try to help Abd El Krim who was fighting against the Spanish. This idea was generally approved but they would need weapons; Garnett solved that problem by borrowing a Winchester repeater from no less than John Galsworthy. In the event the two revolutionary fighters got no further than Algiers, and without their weaponry which had been removed by the Customs Officers in Gibraltar.

Meanwhile Garnett developed and rehearsed and honed his jailbreak plan, which in the event would have done credit to the Cosa

Nostra. He went often to see Sarvarkar in jail, and found out that once a week he had to be taken in a taxi to Bow Street, for renewed remand proceedings. Garnett observed that there was a double gate system at Brixton, operated by a single porter. This process took just long enough, while the car was between doors, for determined attackers to release the prisoner, transfer him to another car and escape. Perhaps the excitement of the scheme is made even greater if one recalls that the kind of vehicles involved were such as in modern times take part in the London Brighton vintage car rally. Garnett rehearsed the details many times over. He found a sympathiser who would provide a car. Pepper sprays would be used to incapacitate the guard. Sarvakar would rapidly be disguised as a woman and driven to the South coast where a specially chartered yacht would take him to France. A small number of dedicated conspirators were briefed and rehearsed which even involved meetings in rowing boats on the Serpentine. An Indian supporter in Paris was charged with chartering the necessary yacht, and funded accordingly. If the whole plan had all the ingredients of a John Buchan or an Erskine Childers thriller all credit goes to the fertile brain of the plan's author; and credit must be redoubled since he had cast himself as the vital man of action from start to finish. He had even thought of recruiting help from the I.R.A. in the person of Maude Gonne, the lady loved by W.B.Yeats.

Action began when Garnett, under the pretence of going to Letchworth where my father had stayed at the artistic colony known as 'The Cloisters', took a train to Paris and met up with the Indian supporter of Savarkar, whose task had been to charter a boat with crew and who had been funded for the purpose.To his chagrin he found that nothing had been done about the boat. He set about the task himself. He could find nothing suitable in Paris, and spent several days without sleep, trying to arrange a yacht in Le Havre. Eventually after much frustration he found a French fishing smack, whose owner agreed to the journey.

A deal was struck, money changed hands and in state of half-starved exhaustion, Garnett returned to the hotel in Paris, where he found his distraught father waiting for him.

The denouement was predictable. Garnett senior escorted him back to Surrey and sanity. He visited Savarkar once more in Brixton and confessed his failure. The Indian leader was hugely grateful for all that he had done and urged him not to feel bad about failure. "It was the intention that truly mattered," he said. In the event he almost made a daring escape on his own. He was charged and taken back to India. At Marseilles he squeezed through a porthole, and being a good athlete managed to swim ashore. But his pursuers caught up with him and he was unable to communicate a request to the Gendarmerie for political asylum. The English Police claimed he was simply a thief. In India he was sentenced to life imprisonment and sent to join my uncle Ullaskar in the Andaman Islands prison camp.

Garnett's withdrawal from political activism ended with his attempt to get back Galsworthy's Winchester which had been taken off my father by Customs officers in Gibralter. He opened a bookshop with Clive Bell, and began serious writing. In his ultimate career he wrote several excellent novels including 'Beaneye', and 'The Sailor's Return', one of the first treatments of race relations in this country. 'Aspects of Love' was made into a Lloyd Weber musical 50 years later. "Lady into Fox" and "A man in the Zoo" became minor classics.

While all this furious adventuring was afoot, my father had settled into a life of calmly pleasurable artistic experience. He had discovered the London theatre and saw several plays and operas. So impressed was he that he decided that the Law as a subject had no interest for him; he must endeavour to found a career on the stage.

During the same period two other experiences had huge emotional impact on him, one of which would be to last for the rest of his life. He was introduced to Opera, and saw several works by Verdi which he felt to be the greatest achievements of which the human psyche was possible. He longed to be able to sing in a manner so sublime. He determined to try.

At the same time, he met in London a lively fresh-faced 18 year old girl from Bristol who had left home under the relentless pressure of parents who had become Seventh Day Adventists. My father fell totally in love with her. For a year or so the two passions were to dovetail. He invited my mother, Ruby Young, to marry him, and join him on a thrilling adventure to Milan, where lived the greatest singing teachers like Maestro Sabatini. She was thrilled by this brown, curly haired young man with his colossal vitality and life-affirming effervescence.

They were married at Paddington Green in 1911 and set out almost at once for Italy.

Ruby Sarah Elizabeth Young

Chapter 3

Proust never had such problems, but lesser mortals often find, when trying to re-call periods of past happiness, they become lost in a golden glow of pleasure, and only the more absurd memories survive.

Among my parents' few dusty souvenirs of Milan were a bronze plaque of Dante, some postcards of the towering interior of La Scala, a black and white print of Botticelli's La Primavera, and a ticket for Milan Football Club. My brother claims our father actually joined it and played on that sacred turf but I have no confirmatory evidence. Nor did I find a cigarette that bears a lipstick's traces. I do however have a most charming testimonial, hand written in Italian to "La Signora Datta" from a chocolate shop called 'Fratelli Munster' where my mother worked to help out their allowance. The date is 1912 and the telephone number is Milan 75.

Nor can one be sure of what Operas they had seen to capture their artistic souls so completely. Verdi most certainly, and some Puccini; But it was so long ago that he, Puccini, had yet to write Turandot. Nor had anyone invented Pizzas.

The bare facts are that they joined a group of mainly foreign singing students, in a setting worthy of 'La Boheme', and my father took lessons from the very best teacher Maestro Sabatini. It must be asked how an Indian, from a totally different musical tradition with its Ragas and melodic quarter tones could respond to Western music with its thundering orchestral power and blazing coloratura singing. One can only suggest that Bengali music, especially that from the river banks, does have a different melodic feel from Indian classical music. And, in any case the Jag Mistrys and the Zubin Mehtas have satisfactorily dealt with such questions.

I have no idea how good a singer my father became; I suspect not very. Of course they all haunted La Scala, and he recounts sadly the end of their dreams. One of their number, a Scotsman, actually won a small part in a production. All packed the Gods in thrilled anticipation of their friend's triumph. But then the worst happened;

he cracked on a high note. The ruthless Italian audience gave him no mercy, hissing and whistling. The group crept home in total dejection. As my father put it;

'He was the best among us. We realised that if he couldn't make it, none of us would. It was time to give up and go home.'

Maestro Sabatini would have to wait a little longer for his new Caruso.

There were at least two valuable consequences of that year in Italy. In order to sing he had to learn how to breathe "through the stomach" as Peter Ustinov lampooned it, so that in later years he could orate like a latter day Demosthenes. A second advantage was that his Italian remained fluent and when he needed to matriculate for Bristol University, he took Physics, Chemistry and Italian. For my mother there was also a taste of her husband's counter-espionage moments; when cycling through Chipping Sodbury they were pursued by a keen constable who had heard them chatting in a strange foreign language and suspected them of being spies.

D.H. Lawrence had a similar experience in Cornwall, but being married to the daughter of the Red Baron himself, he was perhaps prepared for the zenophobia of true patriots. However in Chipping Sodbury not too many people would have known the Italians were on our side.

Failure to capture the world of Opera was accompanied by a factor causing them to think even more seriously of alternatives; my mother was expecting a baby.

As David Garnett embarked on a steady career as a writer, and opened a bookshop with Clive Bell, the doors of the London literary scene gently closed behind them. They made for Bristol and a parental house which offered a warm welcome, but with a total embargo on every kind of indulgence from coffee to secular music.

The bosom of the family was laced straight with leather thongs like the ones my grandfather used on his milkman's horse. It was a roof; with true parental help, but no long term future for people with lively minds. One could hardly blame them for having chosen to spend some of the War to end all Wars lotus-eating in Italy. My father would have decided that if Europeans wished to massacre each other by the million, it was nothing to do with him. If the grandchildren of Queen Victoria chose to send their own people to bayonet each other in the snows of Russia or the mud of Flanders, it was hardly a good example to set the natives of the Empire who they claimed to be trying to teach civilised behaviour. In any case the last time Indians had been involved in anything like a war was 1857 and in that one my great grandfather had been on the side of the Moguls rather than the British.

They returned to an England of fatherless families, brotherless sisters, and one legged cripples selling matches on street corners. The smiling, chin-up bravery of Rupert Brooke had been replaced by the despair of Wilfred Owen and the disgust of Siegfried Sassoon. Even so the great British Empire seemed to have survived it all and perhaps grown mightier yet. George Saxe-Coburg-Gotha had changed his name to Windsor, and survived the deadly onslaught of his cousin Kaiser Wilhelm. Unfortunately he did not quite have the strength of character to save his other cousin, the Tsarina Alexandra and her husband Nicholas, who were dispatched by Bolshevik bullets.

But those still loyal to the concept of Imperial greatness could clearly see how the Dominions and Colonies had rallied to the support of the motherland. No need for late arriving Americans or Russians to secure victory. Australians and Canadians had put aside their often profound contempt for the 'Poms' and 'Jellybags' and sent their boys to fall to Turkish guns at Gallipoli or Bavarian machine gunners on the Somme. Men like Menzies and Massey and McKenzie King could equal Winston Churchill in their devotion to the Union flag and the incumbents of Buckingham Palace. The South Africans gave qualified support through Smuts, and such were British casualties that even Indian mercenaries were sent to wind up their mud and blood-stained puttees in Flanders, and die of pneumonia. Truly, as Haig had said, "There are more of us than there are of them, so we must win."

And he did for them all with his plan of attack.

The Royal Navy too managed to escape back from Jutland to Scapa Flow, with many dreadnaughts still intact. "Something wrong with our ships today" Beattie had said. But perhaps it was just the absence of Nelson. Meanwhile we even held our own in the new style air wars, and D.H. Lawrence's father-in-law Baron Von Richtofen died in his Triplane in 1917.

Empire seemed indestructible, and there was even a handsome English Officer called Eden who emerged unscathed from the trenches and would go on to build a political career that would allow him to preside over the last gasp of Empire at Suez thirty years later in 1956.

My brother was just three years old during the Armistice Day celebrations, and when much older had cause to complain that while all the other children were waving Union Jacks, my father had given him a green flag. He was not to know that "a Terrible Beauty had been born" in a Dublin Post Office, and my father strongly sympathised with Irish Nationalism. The presence of Ireland did however make herself felt in a rather different manner, where my mother's sister Mabel had fallen in love with an impressive Dubliner called Sammy Joyce. This was a sub plot which wove itself into the life my father had now begun to build for wife and child. Dreams of Thespis had been put aside, and he decided that a career in medicine would meet his emotional inclinations, and put bread on the table. Accordingly he took a Matriculation exam for Bristol University, having been allowed as a 21year old to sit at the back of a class at Cotham Grammar School, and catch up on the science and maths he had foregone. He passed in Italian without difficulty, but his proudest moment was when he offered his maths teacher an alternative way to prove Pythagoras' Theorem.

His Irish brother in law was, most surprisingly, a firebrand Seventh Say Adventist, and he held my grandmother's family in thrall. To adjust to such a background after living amongst liberal intellectuals with ultra sophisticated artistic sensitivities must have taken every ounce of my father's conciliatory skills. In that house there was only one book: The Good One. All forms of entertainment were inventions of the Devil who stalked about seeking whom he might devour, after first seducing them with the offer of a cup of tea, and perhaps a cigarette. Even I can recall being corrected by my grandmother for wishing her a "Merry Christmas." 'No, no, David, a Happy Christmas, that's the proper thing to say'. No wonder her daughter had left home.

It remains a puzzle to me how Catholic Ireland could produce a son who hated Rome, and firmly believed the Pope to be a re-incarnation of Satan. Only my father's profound sense of family could have seen him through such discordance. Perhaps the very hard concentration necessary for a medical degree helped him blot out the visions of hell that so beset him round. For all that, Uncle Sammy had a certain appealing quality for which a freethinker could forgive him much. He was a sandy haired Dubliner, probably with genes that harked back to the Vikings. He smiled a lot and even made jokes about Beliefs. His most admirable moment was when he said to my father. 'Shu, if we would combine your talents with my beliefs, we could move Heaven and the Devil!'

Uncle Sammy's 1920 wedding photograph at 21 Ashley Road has twenty one people in it, the older ladies all with proper floral bonnets. One of them was of special interest to my mother. Her Aunt Polly, nee Hatherell Young, had given her five pounds to help her run away to London. She was the last member of her family to have been born at Little Sodbury Manor, where the family had lived for many generations. It was a proud connection indeed. Little Sodbury was a seemingly age old Cotswold Manor, full of charm and replete with history. It was old when Henry VIII had taken Anne Boleyn there, and Elizabeth I also stopped over en route for Bristol. The whole mythology of the place in my mother's imaginings gave rise to thoughts of aristocratic connections, and perhaps even a coat of arms. Alas, later research showed that they had probably merely been tenant farmers there. James Hatherell Young's diary of 1800 showed him to be rather too fond of cider and rum. But it was known that William Tyndale, translator of the bible in 1525 had lived there, and one diary entry records the payment of a fee for medical treatment to the local doctor, Edward Jenner. who was busy developing vaccination theory and practice at Berkeley.

My mother showed distinct signs of her Cotswold origins. She was a big boned, strongly built lass and spoke with the modified West Country accent common in Bristol and not at all unattractive. Her early photographs show a longish acquiline nose that probably owed something to a certain Welsh 'Granny Williams'. In fact it was the kind of face most favoured by quattro centro painters in Italy, like Giotto or Mantegna. While there, a German opera student had fallen quite strongly for her, an event she sometimes liked to tease my father with. She had a wonderful glossary of local phrases too, which she used quite devastatingly with crinkled, smiling light brown eyes.

'You never miss the water till the well runs dry,' was a favourite echo of Little Sodbury life. 'Handsome is as handsome does,' was another gentle comment if anyone told her how attractive her children were. If a family dispute arose she would say 'least said soonest mended', and if it continued "Never let the sun go down on your wrath" which had a forbidding biblical ring. But one of the most memorable carried echoes of maritime history. Once when I was sitting legs sprawled out, she said,

'Square your yards, my son.'

'What did you say Nana?' I asked with astonishment.

'Oh, it's just a saying. It means pull your feet in.'

'But that's got to do with sailing,' I said, 'Something to do with tall ships and Yardarms and such like.'

Then she admitted that as a little girl she had often gone down to the city docks, chatted up one of the sea captains, and gone sailing across the Bristol Channel. She had a spirit of adventure that was quite the equal of my father's.

The family's income derived solely from her father's milk

round. I was once shown the stable where the horse had lived, in a smelly mews off Picton Street. He drove it every day up what was called "Pig Sty Hill", and collected the milk which he distributed all round their home in Ashley Road, a decaying Regency terrace. My mother inherited the property but sold it to her young brother Uncle Willy for £600. He seemed to spend most of his life cycling to Somerset to fish the Avon and Kennett canal.

Of my grandfather I have only the briefest recall. A photo shows him to have had a certain nobility in profile; a little like C. Aubrey Smith who played British generals in Hollywood movies. But there the similarity ended. In advanced senility he took to chasing me under the table, stamping and growling, so that I had to be rescued.

Chapter 4

Determined application to medical study leaves little time for politics. But my father knew enough of Marx to accept the theory of Class Conflict, and he believed firmly that the October Revolution was showing the way forward to a world without the "contradictions" of the capitalist system. The Dictatorship of the Proletariat must surely lead ultimately to the greatest good of the greatest number. The capitalist Imperialist world would contain the seeds of its own destruction.

In India, British rule had already reached its Nadir with the massacre of Amritsar in 1917, when the infamous General Dyer had opened fire on a meeting in an enclosed walled garden, killing more than 300 people. No credit there to the city of Bristol, his home town. Here Empire building had gone from the greatest of pirates, Blackbeard himself, to eighteenth century privateering, with the ships of Woodes Rogers on his world voyage, to steady incomes from full time slavery. One of my favourite little gems was the excursion of General Sir William Draper who brought his force back from India via the Phillippines, conquered them and then sold them back to the Spanish for a sum that set him up in his new Mansion in Bristol most comfortably.

Jane Austen's elegant characters in neighbouring Bath talk much about relative fortunes; but the origins of many of these must surely have come from seafaring Bristol, with its bloodthirsty Captains, swaggering generals and bullying plantation owners. Only rarely does the lady allow them to cast their shadows over the Assemblies, and never in specific detail. Even her own father however, did the accounts for the notorious Warren Hastings in India itself.

In the post war years, home grown industrial conflict was beginning to take shape, and my father would have been well aware of the facts in his liberal newspapers like The News Chronicle and Reynolds News, the great organ founded by the Co-Op pioneers. Class conflict would have seemed inevitable, and the tentative attempts by Lloyd George to limit the powers of the House of Lords, or to bring in state welfare schemes would have seemed like the feeble reforms of someone whom Lenin would have regarded as a typical British bourgeois apologist.

In 1920 my father achieved his M.B.Ch. B. degree and such was his confidence as an examinee that he went on to take a "Medicini Doctor", a higher qualification, the equivalent of a Ph.D, which earned him a permanent place on the University Senate. Here, particularly among the Physicists, he would meet many confirmed Communists.

In 1922 he applied for and gained the post of Medical Officer of Stapleton Hospital. At that time it was a mental hospital, having begun life as a French Prison, changed to a Workhouse, then to an Asylum, finally achieving the dignity of a Geriatric Institution. In its history one could read the whole history of changing British social attitudes over two centuries.

To be a doctor in a mental hospital was not exactly a prestigious appointment; but he accepted it with enthusiasm. An Indian in private medicine at that time was an unknown quantity; he welcomed the security of a State appointment; and in the long run it would allow him to pursue local politics.

Having a devoted English wife and two sons of partly Indian 'extraction' he inclined strongly towards 'Englishness' in his daily habits and pursuits. Indians have a term 'Brown Sahib', which they apply to any of their number who behaves thus. It became most manifest in dress. I always coveted his Harris tweed Norfolk jacket that I found in a wardrobe, and was disappointed that it was too small for me. In fact I almost never saw him dressed in anything other than a three piece suit, the middle class order of the day. Dress considerations bring into focus a certain charming ambivalence. As a socialist he was of course bound to favour the Co-op. He patronised the tailoring department of the Co-op too; but he had suits made to measure. At times he must have been their only customer with such a predilection. But true socialists wish to raise standards not debase them. From Shaw to John Mortimer there are glittering examples of the principle. In later years my father was also extremely proud of his uniform as an "Officer Brother of the Order of St. John of Jerusalem", which he wore frequently during the war.

He was about 5ft.7" in height, which was about the average for English males of his generation. He had three brothers including Ullaskar, all of whom were somewhat taller. Photographs of my grandfather show him to have been a very handsome man with a short beard that gave him a remarkable resemblance to George Vth. His father was an orthodox Hindu and strongly disapproved of his son's choice of a marriage partner, a girl of a different caste with whom he had fallen passionately in love. It was probably from her that my father inherited curly hair and a complexion darker than most Brahmins. He took great care over his appearance, and each morning one could hear the steady clatter of his Rolls Razor in the bathroom. This was a luxurious piece of equipment which came in an oblong chromium plated box containing a "stropping" mechanism to give the sharpest possible blade every day.

His given name was the Bengali "Sukh Sagar", meaning "Ocean of sweetness". This lent itself neatly to his English nickname of "Sugar",which I heard for most of his life, although my mother normally shortened this to "Shu". In all languages his name suited his disposition perfectly.

I became aware from my most tender years that I was in some essential way 'different' from those children about me. My distinctiveness occupied a certain stratum of consciousness, like an ozone layer in one's awareness, that one was never far from being conscious of. There were remarkably few taunts from other children; immigrants were a total rarity in Britain at that time. West Indians were almost unknown, except for one who ran a sweetshop in Fishponds, which was dubbed the 'Black Man's shop'. A few others attended the University and then returned home. I doubt if there were more than half a dozen families of Indian, or part Indian extraction, like the Jahans, Godivalas and Mohans in a city of nearly half a million.

But I had only to catch sight of my father walking across the 'Green' from his office to be reminded that I, his son, was different from the other kids. So did that mean I had a problem? I can categorically answer "no", at least in my pre-pubescent years. The reason for that is not far to seek, and it has a tripartite causality.

In England between the wars, social standing mattered almost above all else. My father was the Stapleton Hospital doctor. He counted for something. He was also a man of such charm and considerateness to all about him that he won universal affection. Whoever needed a kind word, or a little help could depend on him for it whether they worked with him, or met him casually.

The second element in my fall back position was my mother. She too radiated a kind of sub-aristocratic concern for the less fortunately placed. There was something traditionally English in her ability to maintain her position, yet offer a qualified friendship for trades people, farm workers and factory hands. It seems to me a flair developed by the English landed gentry over the years that had probably ensured there would never be a French Revolution in these islands. She acted the part beautifully with all those she met, and they loved her for it. It also meant that she could help my father to create a warm, secure environment with manifest feelings of love for both of her children; for me especially, the younger son by twelve years. Unquestionably I was spoilt: it probably sapped my ambition and resolve as I grew older, but it utterly assuaged any other problems I might have when growing up.

The third element in my motte and bailey defence, was the almost castle-like house where I was born and named 'David' (after my father's first English friend, Garnett, by now a respected author).

Snowdon House was built of stone quarried nearby, giving it three foot thick walls, and it stood alone in sixty acres of farmland. It had three storeys and Queen Anne Windows, around which wound two Virginia creepers, which blazed deep red in autumn. There was an oak beamed, low ceilinged lounge, dining and sitting room, which had probably once been two separate rooms. In this lay clues to a much greater age than its windows suggested because one corner boasted an oak settle typical of the 17th century, and the glass fronted case which housed my mother's china collection, must have been an inglenook fireplace, with a built-in window seat alongside. The lower windows with vestigial Tudor lintels also confirmed the greater age of the earliest part, which originally must have been a farmhouse. The extra floor would have been added at the time of the American Wars of Independence, when Stapleton Institution had originally been built to house French, Spanish and American prisoners of war. Snowdon House itself would probably have been used to accommodate senior officers.

On the West wall of the lounge a door led out to a verandah, itself a rather American touch, and on the South side a further door opened into a huge glass conservatory where my mother grew much prized chrysanthemums. Two further smaller ground floor rooms were used, one as a study, the other was a small dining room, adjacent to the kitchen with its stone flagged floor, with an antiquated kitchen range. All rooms had fireplaces, and two of them needed to be kept burning throughout the winter. They were fed from a deep coal cellar, reached by stone steps. In this there were remnants of a tunnel which had been bricked up; perhaps a memento of an early attempt at escape.

To this estate agent's description, I can only add one element that is purely hypothetical, and a notion entirely of my own. Not only had the house added a storey (to give it six bedrooms) it had, during its history, performed a unique and quite remarkable 'about turn'.At what was, in our time the back of the house, was a massive old door, strongly nailed in place and hidden by a velour curtain. This would have opened to face the staircase, as one would have expected. What we now knew as the 'front' door would originally have been a smaller 'back' door. So that if one entered and wished to climb up the stairs, one had to perform an 'about turn'. None of us commented on this oddity at the time, but in retrospect, the 'about turn' theory is the only feasible one. The house had originally been built to face the City of Bristol in the West; but since then a road called Snowdon Road had been built on the East side, and Snowdon House had had to turn round to face it.

All such considerations aside, it was a wonderful old house in which to spend the first twenty years of one's life. Its solid walls and impressive aspect gave one a psychological armour against the rest of the world. It was a fortress fit for a self appointed young princeling and few external attacks could weaken my moral ramparts.

The ground it stood in was a further defence. Rolling acres were what every British aristocrat aspired to, and Snowdon House had a sufficiency of them. Half a dozen men came to plough the fields and scatter. And I woke every morning to the sound of the hooves of one or more magnificent Shire horses clopping up the lane, and being sworn at in purest Anglo-Saxon as they were backed into the traces. The produce provided basic life and limb subsistence for up to 700 patients; potatoes, cabbages, and patches of swede and rhubarb in tall 'forcing' pots. Only once I recall a corn harvest; a genuine steam engine clanking up the hill, towing a hugely complicated threshing machine, the whole performance collecting a throng of excited admirers, with all the sounds and smells familiar to Thomas Hardy's Bathsheba.

At a safe olefactory distance from the house was a substantial piggery where Gloucestershire 'Old Spots' met their doom. As a child I queried why the little piggies made such a squealing noise on some mornings. My mother shielded me from the truth with a perfectly reasonable explanation.

'They're squealing because they want their breakfast,' was quite acceptable. Only when I matured enough to pay them a visit and saw the instruments of slaughter hanging on the walls, did the truth reveal itself. "Breakfast" was certainly relevant; "Not where they eat, but where they are eaten". As Hamlet himself said.

Finally to complete this idyll of self-sufficiency was the orchard. Walled of course and occupying at least an acre, it contained dozens of pear, cherry, plum and apple trees, with long lines of gooseberries, white, red, and black currants. There were three large greenhouses heated by coke fuelled boilers which provided tomatoes for much of the year.

In charge of all this was Mr. Wines, an amiable Head Gardener with a walrus moustache, who posed proudly for his photograph sitting on a prize winning pumpkin. On cold winter mornings he would knock on my mother's door bearing some choice vegetables, and be rewarded by a mug of hot cocoa.

With this whole sense of prestige and gracious living surrounding me it is hardly surprising that I grew up feeling like some young aristo rather than a social oddity. If, has been suggested, our illusions are our most cherished possessions, then all through childhood, puberty and adolescence, my illusions were all encompassing.

For the simple truth of the matter is is that we owned none of it.

Not one single gooseberry from the orchard was ours, and certainly our very home, dear old Snowdon House, did not belong to us. No Great Gatsby, no 'Grande Meaulnes', ever cherished such a fantasy as I did. And probably I could not have survived without it.

At this point one cannot avoid plunging into a reverie which belongs firmly in the literary genre that embraces Candleford and Penny Hassett.

The house was on high ground and below it there wound a sluggish little river called the Frome, which rose somewhere at the foot of the Cotswolds. Close to the house, at a place called Snuff Mills, it passed through a miniature gorge, precipitous and densely wooded. The walk along it, once taken by the famed cricketer W.G. Grace, was exquisitely pastoral. On the skyline to the North stood the noble house of the Dowager Duchess of Gloucester. In a spot called Wickham Glen was a group of old houses which, history tells us were used by Cromwell and Fairfax in their siege of Bristol.

Even in recent years, in spite of the Howard's End invasion of housing estates and a vicious Motorway, I have taken people along it and watched them melt in the natural charm of the place.

The National Trust fights hard to save what is left; and it is a great sadness that that can no longer include Snowdon House, which fell victim to the Council planners of the fifties and their compulsion to build wherever the grass is greenest. Reports told that it took two cranes, swinging their concrete weights in tandem, to knock down the thick stone walls that protected me for twenty one years.

Suffice to say that I re-call a moment, an hour even, that truly merits the term 'euphoria'. Lying on my back in the long grass, Labrador patiently waiting, I gazed into the endlessly blue Summer sky, with skylarks calling and asked, "Could there ever be happiness greater than this? Could any moment hereafter equal the bliss of this endless blue depth, this pure heaven of pleasure?"

But walk half a mile in the other direction and the City had already swallowed up the Parish of Fishponds with its schools, library, station, and above all the Vandyke Cinema where the joys of cowboy films and Buck Rogers seduced our mind every Saturday for fourpence a go. We were also lucky enough to have one of the first Woolworth's in the area, an Ali Baba cave of temptations priced at 3d or 6p per purchase. One of all the delights on offer, the fountain pens drew one time and again, each an explosion of whirling liquid colours in wonderful Bakelite that seemed to herald a whole new concept of civilization. Only a cliche like the 'best of all possible worlds' could encapsulate an adolescent's feelings about living in such an area.

Nor did it give any hint of being too good to last; which of course it was.

To belong to the comfortable car owning middle-class in the mid-thirties seemed almost the ultimate that human experience could offer. We drove where we wanted, picnic hampers dominated, traffic was light, we holidayed wherever we chose in the British Isles.

My parents formed a close friendship with my mother's cousin who had become a librarian in Pontypridd, and a man of some renown in the Rhondda. Uncle Wilf Cowdrey was a jovial character and we exchanged visits with him and Auntie Naomi several times a year.

The journey was like a foreign adventure. There were no bridges into Wales, and we had to join the queue of cars at Aust where they were packed with amazing skill into one of the two ferry boats, the Severn King and Queen. Our taste of South Wales was more foreign than France. It was a world of pit-wheels and slagheaps and Bethel Chapels. There seemed to be coal everywhere. Men with mufflers and caps walked with their collie dogs in the middle of the road. Many were unemployed and my father could experience at first hand all the problems that would confirm his socialist theories in practice. My Uncle's proudest boast was that he took over a library in which there were no books, only players of cribbage. Within five years he had filled it with books and the gamblers were reading hard, as though each determined to become a Richard Llewellyn or a Dylan Thomas.

From the mid-twenties onwards, though we were barely conscious of it, we were all involved in the greatest revolution of all; one which had little to do with theory or political power; it was the seizure of the soul of mankind by the internal combustion engine.Up to then only the very rich had had their de Dions and Silver Ghosts. But now Henry Ford and William Morris put cars within reach of a middle class that comprised a substantial slice of the population. Trams, trains and bicycles were still the only transport for the majority; but now Austins, Fords and Morrises appeared in such numbers that traffic lights and Halt signs had become essential.

Toad of Toad Hall, whooping with delight, had shown those with steady incomes all the joys of the open road and the only hazards were horse drawn carts and herds of cows. Today's mass market obsession with marques and performance factors, satellite navigation and high speed brakes began with gentlemanly discussions about Lagondas and Lanchesters, and how far they would be likely to get before breaking a spring or boiling on a hot day. In those days even main roads had ditches deep enough to trap the unwary. My father's first car was an almost mythical product called a Calthorpe. It was chain driven and thus merited an early demise. He replaced it with a car that acquired almost legendary status, a 'Bull nosed' Morris.

Then in the early thirties a different marque caught his attention; smaller, much faster and with several technological advances that appealed to him. The 'Riley Nine' was a fabric bodied competitor to the Austin Seven but offered more exclusivity. The fabric body was soon abandoned, probably due to its flammability, and it was replaced by a most attractive Riley range that included the Falcon, Kestrel and Adelphi. They were sleek, had lower profiles and semi-automatic gear boxes that gave them a more sporting image than the Rovers of the day. My father fell for a 1936 Adelphi, regarded as a 'poor man's Lagonda,' that took us in style to Cornwall, Snowdonia, Scarborough and the Scottish Highlands. He kept it for eleven years, long enough for me to borrow for my first 'pub crawl', a reprehensible activity now totally and with good reason, forbidden.

Of all the trips we made in pursuit of holiday pleasures, none had quite the traumatic effect on me as the rare, but epoch making journeys to London. Already one had become aware that all the truly important things that happened, took place in the capital city. If my father had political occasions there, like an India League meeting, or a medical course (he took part of his Diploma in Psychiatric Medicine there) he would travel by the "Bristolian" express train to Paddington. The journey by car was a major undertaking along the old A4, and took well over four hours. Normally we chose to avoid Bath and would skirt the Cotswolds via Marshfield, then on to Chippenham and Calne, where the sausages came from. With luck we would make Marlborough for coffee and perhaps find ourselves sitting at a table near Betjeman's "thumping cad" chatting up his lady. Otherwise we would pull in for a picnic break in Savernake Forest, so that the driver could be restored for the next leg to Reading. All along the route the most reassuring sight was that of the AA Patrolmen in their yellow livery and sidecars, who gave smart salutes to our proudly displayed badge. My father never failed to return their salutes.

By the time that Reading invited us to join its excruciating crawl, we knew we were far from home, then Maidenhead extended us a similar courtesy. After that, if the radiator behaved itself we could tackle the endless traffic lights of Slough's industrial estates, hoping to hit them in a lucky sequence of green after green. By Chiswick, fatigued but excited, the acrid smell of London's electric trains and breweries was upon us. We were in London. In Piccadilly or Trafalgar Square I became starry eyed at the sight of so much wealth on show. Every male wore a bowler hat, every woman looked as though she were on the way to a ball, and every car seemed to be a Rolls Royce. Many in fact were, but I learned to distinguish them from the equally hearse-like Beardmore Taxis. The shops were paradisal in their offerings. One wanted to die and go to Gamages, where model trains raced around under real flying model aeroplanes. But my mother with her provincial loyalties never made self indulgent requests to see Bond Street. Back in Bristol there was always Baker Baker's and the Co-Op. She knew her milieu.

The London experience would never fade. It seeped into the psyche, and I sensed that one day I would have to go and live there, even if I had to become a weary commuter grinding in each day from some grimy inner suburb.

***

However it was much more than cars and a high quality of life that made my father embrace England so enthusiastically. It was above all the high regard for progressive thinking, which led him to love the English language itself. He spoke without an accent, and soon began to forget his native Bengali almost completely. He read avidly. He had a special book rest made, and many evenings would find him in a 'Wing' chair, buried in anything from a work of Karl Marx to a novel by Thackeray or Trollope. He knew his Dickens and his Shakespeare well, and most of the major English poets He also greatly admired Victor Hugo and Emile Zola. But he loved humour above all, and would quote from Mark Twain as well as from his adored Socialist mentor George Bernard Shaw. His favourite jest was to greet all medical problems with "Stimulate the Phagocytes!"

a line from "The Doctor's Dilemma"

All this allowed him facility with sayings like "Fine words butter no parsnips" (flung at rival politicians) and "Honest sweat makes smelly pants," his version of the Royal motto, "Honi Soi Qui Mal Y Pense." Like any true Brown Sahib he regarded integration as a privilege and a duty, especially when it gave scope for humour.

Snowdon House included a large room at the top where he religiously kept all his copies of the British Medical Journal, which he considered required professional reading. There was also a corner in which were stored many copies of his father's works of Hindu philosophy, printed by an antiquated Calcutta letterpress. The rest of the family would have regarded them as oddities, if not an actual embarrassment, but he would have read them all. The main function of the room was to provide a place in which my brother and his fiancee could practice their dance steps in Hollywood musical style. Their Bible was the best selling manual on Ballroom Dancing by Victor Sylvester, which showed exactly where to place the feet, in Quickstep, Slow Foxtrot, or Tango. A wind up gramophone provided the music and there were records by the man himself (which as a jazz fan I learned to hate).

I could just about tolerate numbers by Harry Roy, and Lew Stone, like "Tiger Rag", but my favourite was a novelty number called "The Laughing Policeman" by a great benefactor of mankind called Penrose.

Sadly, the records of Caruso, Pinza and Amelita Galli-Curci were rarely played.

Chapter 5

War having proved the ultimate lunacy, British patriotic urges needed a new outlet. They found it in World Record breaking which became the nation's prime pre-occupation during the twenties and thirties.

The Blue Riband was the accolade given for the fastest Atlantic crossings and in due course this became a duel between the French and the British whose 'Queen Mary' achieved the satisfaction of beating their Gallic neighbour's 'Normandie' with a record that held until the outbreak of the Second world war. Perhaps most valuably, the building of such great ships brought high employment levels to the Clyde, though not to Jarrow

On the permanent way, steam locomotives reached speeds at which Stevenson's friends would have though it impossible for the human frame to survive. The LNER Mallard reached 126 mph., as fast as many airliners. The love affair with the motor car became climactic with heroes like Sir Henry Segrave and Sir Malcolm Campbell, Eyston and Cobb. They saw off all competition even from the U.S.A., and every male child needed to have a lead model of Campbell's famous 'Bluebird'.

The most celebrated road race in Europe was that of Le Mans. To win it became an obsession of the European upper classes and the British produced the well breeched competitors who could guarantee our supremacy. The car they opted for was the enormous, rugged workhorse designed by W.O. Bentley. For six whole years no foreigner would match it though Italian and French designers like Bugatti must have prayed fervently for a car to equal it.

The bravest of pioneers however must have been those who took to the air in their flimsy craft that sometimes seemed to offer little advance on the one that first flew at Kittyhawk.

Unquestionably the name that ruled in the firmament was that of Amy Johnson. Born in Hull she became the first woman to fly from England to Australia in 1930 in a Gipsy Moth monoplane; she also broke her own husband's record to South Africa. The most popular song of the day had the refrain,

"Amy, wonderful Amy....."

At the same time, in Southampton came a presage of future national drama. A man called Schneider had awarded a cup for aerial speed records. The contest was entered exclusively by seaplanes, and the British won it on four occasions. The last victory at a speed of 320 mph in 1931 was in a plane powered by a wonderful Rolls Royce engine called a 'Merlin' and designed by one R.J. Mitchell. In subsequent years its design would form the basis of a fighter plane to be known as the 'Spitfire'.

In sport and athletics the nation was less dominant, but heroes existed nevertheless. Adolf Hitler had espoused the Olympic Games as a means of proving German superiority. The world applauded when a black American Jesse Owens, overwhelmed all competition as a sprinter. In fact this was the start of world domination by blacks rather than whites which seems to have continued. British efforts were no more successful than the Germans. but we did record one notable success; Harold Abrahams, a sprinter who won the 100 yards 'dash' in 1924.

By far the most famous sporting name in the mid thirties was that of Fred Perry who won Wimbledon for three consecutive years. And in the nationally obsessive game of cricket, taken to the farthest corners of the Empire, the Test match battle with Australia became so all-important that there was talk of breaking off diplomatic relations over English Captain Jardine's use of the 'bodyline' fast bowler Harold Larwood in the 1932 series.

The great function of all this emphasis on national achievement was to take minds off soup kitchens and dole queues wherever they existed. God was in his heaven, and all was well in Britain and even an unemployed Welsh miner could take pride in the fact that Tommy Farr had come close to beating Joe Louis.

It is perhaps a matter of wonder in our Television age when we are bombarded with images of the allegedly famous, that a whole nation could be kept at such a fever pitch of excitement.

Newspapers had reached new heights of appeal and distribution, but it was Radio that could do all that Television does, without a single picture; except for those in the imagination. People even huddled around their radios as though proximity to the air waves stimulated mental images in the brain. Which of course it does. All this must be attributed to the foster child of the great Lord Reith, the British Broadcasting Corporation. As democrats we feel vastly superior to lesser nations with their State broadcasting networks to control their subjects. Lord Reith chose subtler methods

The BBC was and is a classic invention based on a cherished notion of independence and freedom of expression. The taxpayer funds it, but Parliament has no say in what it does. And yet, the BBC in those years exercised a power over its listeners that ensured that the viewpoint of the establishment was maintained at all times.

Those recruited to run it were drawn almost exclusively from Public Schools and Oxbridge, so that the greatness of the British Empire was never likely to be called into question. Censorship was endemic, unspoken, and every programme had an accent, quite literally, that allowed no question about Royalty, or the essential goodness of the British way of life. It was the most cohesive force that any nation could have.

It began with the Announcers. These, the great celebrities of the day, addressed their listeners, whatever their social standing, in accents originating somewhere between Mayfair and Oxford, favouring a high nasal tone, pompous, patronising and almost always male. All wore Dinner jackets. And how we loved them. The Howard Marshalls, Stuart Hibberds and Freddie Grisewoods were part of the family; like eldest sons who had done rather well and might even have met Royalty. Yes, they were snobs, but every Englishman has a little secret watch pocket in which he keeps his social climbing ambitions.

News was news. We were told precisely what was good for us, and the notion of 'investigative journalism' would have caused a fit of vapours in Portland Place.

At Christmas especially, these wonderful voices brought us

messages from the farthest reaches of the Empire, with memorable phrases like "Come in Southern Rhodesia", or "Can you hear us in Darwin?". And everyone from Penang to Vancouver was eating Christmas Pudding. Radio entertained us quite magically. If the Home Service was for 'serious matters', The Light Programme did full justice to that proudest of faculties - the English sense of humour. My Mother loved Gillie Potter's chat to us about the doings in his mythical country village of Hogsnorton, which she swore was really Chipping Sodbury, and Stainless Stephen voiced the stoical acceptance of Northern industrial life.

The supremacy of the upper crust was maintained in the public school tones of Flotsam and Jetsam, while Clapham and Dwyer were permitted to be only slightly down the social scale. My father was most keen on Billy Bennett who delivered mock heroic monologues, and played an instrument of his own invention, the 'phono-fiddle'. Elsie and Doris Waters, favoured just slightly London accents in their family sketches; but my mother drew the line at Doris Hare, whom she found sometimes far too vulgar.

When not at his books, my father's great pleasure was listening to the BBC while slowly peeling a post prandial apple, or rather more indulgently producing innocent clouds of smoke from one of his then favoured cigarettes, "Greys", in their expensive tins, or the exotically oval "Passing Clouds." Nicotine was one of the Lord's great gifts to man.

In time, another minor addiction became apparent, as the nation was gripped by Football Pools. My father succumbed to this harmless activity, and catching the post on a Friday became vitally important. But though he loved a glass of sherry, my mother's frown ensured that he restricted all forms of alcohol to the Christmas period.

The Beeb did very well by musicians of the day, giving full air time to Henry Hall, Carrol Gibbons and Geraldo, while the Palm Court Orchestra had a regular Sunday evening spot. Sir Henry Wood's Promenade Concerts began in 1927, and the BBC formed its own Symphony Orchestra three years later. Perhaps the biggest listening audiences were those that gravitated to the variety programmes that helped to soothe the cares of each new working week. In Town Tonight was an acceptably mild form of the celebrity cult, while 'Monday night at Seven' (later 'Eight') and ultimately Arthur Askey's 'Bandwagon', gave us sketches, comedy spots, and puzzle corners for all tastes.

Full justice was done to the theatrical tradition and offered memorable performances of Dickens adaptations. The radio serial would have been invented in the late twenties, and there was one that living actors continue to praise. Once a week I leapt on my bike at 4.30 from school and cycled the six or so miles home at a furious pace in time to hear the stentorian tones of Norman Shelley as Professor Challenger in Conan Doyle's "The Lost World". So gripping was the performance that my father closed his office early and walked home to hear it. It was a special moment of family bonding, and I know he could have forgiven the British Empire all its transgressions for making it possible for our senses and spirits to enjoy such fictional nourishment.

"Pterodactyls !" shouted Professor Challenger, and so initiated the world's obsession with Dinosaurs. The voice of Norman Shelley was legendary, and it is even rumoured that he stood in for Winston Churchill in some of his famous wartime broadcasts rallying the nation.

There was one programme above all whose memory is likely to bring on tears of nostalgia. "Children's Hour" featured a seemingly eternal series called "Toytown." Listeners imaginations ranged free over this purely verbal location populated by characters like Larry the Lamb, Dennis the Dachshund, and the irascible Lord Mayor, Mr. Grouser, facing problems which somehow always contrived to permit good natured solutions.

But the Beeb's greatest achievement must have been its part in lifting the spirit of the nation in wartime with Tommy Handley's surrealist show ITMA. Whole families could sit and forget about Hitler while chuckling at the inane voices of "Funf" the spy, and the "Can I do you now sir ?" of Mrs Mop, the cleaning lady. ITMA created the whole genre of fantasy comedy that has fathered all radio and TV to the eras of Milligan, Cleese and their many brilliant peers.

If the BBC dominated entertainment, the lure of Hollywood still brought people away from their firesides. Local cinemas not only provided boys with the chance to kill Indians on Saturday afternoons at fourpence a go; it was for many people a regular weekly venue for the whole family. My father indulged us and suffered glossy Hollywood comedies or Busby Berkeley stage sets, or Fred Astaire and Ginger Rogers, in extravaganzas designed for hand holding lovers. But he longed for something of greater social significance, and finally it happened with 'Grapes of Wrath'. For him it was the greatest movie ever made, perhaps because it showed how even the homeland of capitalist enterprise could at times subject its people to the life lived by a landless peasant in his own country. In his eyes, Henry Fonda was the best film actor in the world.

But my mother had little time for film stars.

'I went to Fairfield School,' she said, 'with this chap, what do they call him, 'Cary Grant'. His real name was Archie Leach. He was always getting into trouble.'

As in all provincial cities the live theatre fought hard to survive, kept alive mainly by prolonged seasons of Pantomime, most lavishly at the huge Hippodrome. And long before the Theatre Royal rediscovered itself as the oldest in the land, the Princes' Theatre made gallant efforts, sometimes putting on Shakespeare or even Ibsen. The whole family was taken to see Shaw's "Arms and the Man" starring Robert Donat. It was a memorable performance, made even more memorable by the fact that not many months after, the Prince's Theatre was reduced to rubble by German bombs.

For me the most poignant memorial in Bristol is in St Stephens Church. After losing his theatre, the manager of the Princes joined the army. He was killed in action.

Chapter 6

If the BBC created a sense of national well-being, social cohesion and contentment, it did so by obfuscating tensions and conflicts in the worlds of politics and labour relations.

Savage reductions in miners' pay in 1925 had led to regular strikes which culminated in the T.U.C's declaration of a General Strike in 1926. Not least among the progenitors of this unprecedented action was Ernest Bevin, the bluff West Country born Secretary of the Transport and General who had once delivered Ginger Beer in Fishponds.

The Labour Party's majority in 1924 had been drastically reduced after Ramsay MacDonald's failure and resignation, and it fell to the Conservative leader Stanley Baldwin to balance the budget and deal with a situation that looked to many like Red Revolution after the Zinoviev letter, and A.J. Cook's declaration that he admired Lenin. For my father to have joined the Labour Party at about this time must have taken quite considerable courage.

It says much for the comfort and security of the middle classes here at the heart of the Empire, that opposition to the General Strike was almost universal. Chaps in plus fours left their cars in order to drive buses, and in 1927 a Trades Disputes Act was passed which made sure nothing like it could happen again. By way of compensation, pensions to widows and the old were increased, and the existence of soup kitchens was limited to unemployment black spots and never for very long periods.

Foremost among the strike's opponents was Winston Churchill whose obsession with the Gold Standard had led to the miners' problems in the first place. The truth must be that it was the continued existence of the Empire that had helped to reduce the effects of recession compared with Germany and the U.S.

Many thousands of people still found work and long term careers, as executives, civil servants or teachers in India, Southern Rhodesia, Nigeria, Singapore and a whole host of countries which still had colonial or protectorate status. Even a radical like George

Orwell found his first job in the Burma Police where he famously had to shoot his elephant and protect the locals. It would have been hard to find a leafy suburban street anywhere in England where at least one family did not have a member gainfully employed abroad beneath the Union Jack. Even the Church of England was a major employer in its humble way, and many writers drew inspiration from Imperial settings. The total balance sheet of Imperial benefits would have to include many of the world's most sought after products, including rubber, tin, tea, cocoa, gold, nickel, timber, and wheat. The jealousy in certain German minds can be imagined.

There were frequent official reminders too of the power of the Empire. 1924 saw a massive Empire Exhibition staged at Olympia, where people bought brass from India, and saw genuine Kayaks as used by North American Indians, who exchanged animal skins for Witney blankets.

It must have been my brother who requested that we go to see an RAF air display at Filton. The high spot of the afternoon was a simulated bombing raid on 'disloyal' villages somewhere in the Middle East. My father would have known the point of it all at once. It wasn't until I was far older and aware of Britain's mighty reach that I understood matters better. The RAF was heavily engaged in the thirties "disciplining" tribesmen in Iraq from their base at Habbaniyah. Eight squadrons were involved, and others were doing much the same in the tribal areas of Afghanistan. British oil supplies and borders had to be secured at all cost; after all, "Russians with snow on their boots" had been seen in North Indian bazaars.

Little did our politicians and military strategists imagine what a stockpile of hatred they were building up in Moslem countries which would cause us such problems in this, the 21st Century. And their naivety was such that a mission was even sent to Japan to help build up the Japanese Air Force; we much favoured them after they had shown they could successfully 'give the Russians a beating' in 1911.

My father's intellectual and political life grew at a steady pace through the late twenties and thirties. His concern was essentially the physical well-being of his patients, most of whom had been certified as insane by the procedures of the day, although there were a large number who were simply inadequate in their daily lives. Some worked on the farm, and one named Draper came to help my mother in Snowdon house. His was a classic case of the "asylum" principle in British society; an orphan, he had been rescued from the streets by the Nuns of St. Joseph's home and when mature he had been passed on to Stapleton for full time care. In the house, he helped with the laying of fires of which there were at least two, and sometimes three kept burning. He tried to help my mother prepare vegetables, but she found he could barely peel a potato successfully, and she had to rescue anything he put his hand to. Most afternoons one would find him dozing by the breakfast room fire, holding a partly read copy of the Catholic Universe. He was famous in Fishponds for going into shops and giving vent to the most fertile stories about all of the rest of us.

Snowdon House had a study with lofty bookcases crammed with volumes. There was plenty of unconventional reading, including Das Kapital, the Marx and Engels letters, The Communist Manifesto, and Dialectical Materialism. Even the works of Hegel found a place there.

Sometimes my father would meet me from school in the Riley, and on the way home stop in the Haymarket for twenty minutes or so when he somewhat furtively entered a shop known as the 'bomb shop', which specialised in left wing literature, emerging with some secretive work promising the demise of capitalism. When adolescent I too made use of the study; not merely for surreptitious glances through Gray's 'Anatomy', but finding Freud's 'Introductory Lectures', a fascinating read on matters of sexual perversion quite beyond the school syllabus. All the left wing works were highly suspect politically since this was well before the outbreak of war when it became briefly fashionable to be pro-Russian. Nevertheless my own left wing values. and vague notions of Communist Theology grew by a process of osmosis, rather than any determined study of my father's books.

Nor did the Devil have it all his own way in my consciousness. My first school at age 5 had been the Infants' school attached to the St. Matthias Training College, and no-one could have had a better introduction to the beliefs and practices of the Church of England. The two ladies who taught us, represented two facets of Christianity; Miss Griffin, angular and Welsh, dinned into us some at least of the Ten Commandments and the Creed; Miss Butter, a plump Devonian, represented love, miracles and gentle Jesus meek and mild. Sin and retribution combined with fellowship and devotion in time- honoured C.of E. style One learnt to pray with eyes clamped painfully shut, knowing that even if one eyelid relaxed, God might stop listening.

Then one day I experienced a blinding proof that God existed. My big brother had been picked to play for Bristol United, at Teignmouth, near Exeter. Proud father decided that we must all go and support him. We would leave at around 11 a.m. for the fifty mile journey. That morning, as the picnic was being prepared, I asked if I could go out to play first. My mother said 'Yes, but only for an hour, at the back of the house.' I went off. Soon I was down by the river. Time had no meaning, as the larks flew high above. Eventually I thought I had better go back. I wandered home. When I reached the drive, I stopped in horror. The car had gone. I ran to the road. It was nowhere to be seen.

The dreadful truth began to strike home. My parents, those people who were supposed to love me so much, had abandoned me. They no longer cared for me. I could starve to death. I could die. My eyes filled with tears, and I began to run wildly about the place, hoping for a glimpse of them. They were nowhere to be seen. I ran back along the path by which I had just returned. Heart pounding I kept running. Then the one slim chance of rescue came to me. If indeed there was a God, and if he loved me, surely he would save me. As I ran, I formulated a prayer. It was a very detailed and specific prayer, namely that as I rounded the next bend, Peggy, my brother's fiancee, would appear, looking for me. Surely God would help me in my torment. So I prayed. And prayed.

And then the miracle happened. Around that very bend came no one other than Peggy, frantically searching for me. My prayer had been answered in every precise detail. I knew then beyond a shadow of doubt that God existed; he cared for us; he answered prayers. It was a conviction that remained deep inside me for many years. It was my conversion on the road to Exeter.

My father's evenings became more and more involved with the Bristol Labour Party, and the T.G.W.U. There can have been few professional men who belonged to the latter, nevertheless intellectuals had become a feature of the left wing. Professor J.B.S. Haldane was a frequent contributor to the Daily Worker and physicists like Blackett were notable supporters. Perhaps their belief in an ordered Universe let them to seek 'laws' of social behaviour of the kind promulgated by Marx. Even George Bernard Shaw bombarded the Times with letters of a deep red hue.

At most of his Labour party branch meetings my father proved to be an excellent chairman. When he did take to open air oratory as he occasionally did on Bristol's speakers' corner, 'The Downs', it was to campaign for Indian Independence, and for a National Health Service .

My mother meanwhile began to feel that politics had 'taken over', and she did not hesitate to complain. Summer afternoons at the Tennis Club seemed long gone, although Summer Holidays and weekend picnics were still very much part of life. In due course she discovered her own interests in handicrafts. In those days evening classes were abundant, and free, and she went out to local schools to pursue ambitious works of embroidery and even metalwork, bringing home useful pewter boxes with retrousse designs. I still use them today.

But a far more serious threat to the family's way of life, came from my father's place of work. Stapleton was still a 'Poor Law' Institution, and so had an administrative head - significantly called 'The Master'. In the early days the 'Master' was a jolly sort of chap called Waters, who had a predilection for entertainment and always organised a Christmas Show in which he played a key role. He also

instituted a cinema with projectionist, and Laurel and Hardy became the inmates' much loved heroes.

Sadly in about 1938 he retired, and his place was taken by a man of dissimilar inclinations. Height about 5'4", weight almost eighteen stone, and with all the charm and sensitivity of a Charles Dickens hate figure. He was also married to the Hospital Matron.

Marching with the Union through Queen Square

Conflicts were inevitable and even though I formed a juvenile friendship with their son, matters came to a head in a serious manner. There were racial insults, and my father came close to breaking point under the daily confrontations. It was only when things got to the point of litigation that my father found enormous support from one of the male nurses, Jim Matthews, who was a politically active member of the Bristol Trades Council. When it became clear that all concerned were teetering on the edge of disaster, my father made a superhuman effort to mend matters. His overture was gratefully accepted. People kept their jobs; lawyers had to seek emoluments elsewhere.

Soon after this my father took a step which has since raised several eyebrows. He became a Freemason. Campaigning Socialists were not common in that weird world of ritualistic male bonding. Explanations have been demanded of me, and his ambivalence is not easy to come to terms with. I believe I may be able to square that circle however. My father formed a profound friendship with another doctor, a general practitioner called Lucas. He was a hugely likeable man, warm and considerate. When I developed a stomach pain it was to Lucas that my father turned at once, valuing his professionalism. He prodded and poked me in the approved manner, and then spoke two words. "Appendix - Southmead". I was admitted for an operation in the nick of time; it was long before the days of Penicillin. And there was another side to Lucas that appealed to my father; he wrote short stories. I remember reading some of them. Though he never became a Maugham, it showed a depth and sensitivity that greatly appealed. My father would have been delighted to join his Lodge, which seemed a harmless activity, and of course might even prove of value if his own professional situation should revert to the confrontational.

Inevitably most of my father's acquaintances were involved in local Labour Party politics They had names that featured strongly in local press correspondence columns like St. John Reade, Ted Rees, the agent, Harry Hennessy a Union heavyweight. There were few local labour M.P's, but eventually Stafford Cripps would become Chancellor of the post war exchequer, and Tony Benn a thorn in the side of all who deviated from manifesto promises.

His natural gregariousness would have been to welcome almost any of these into Snowdon House, but he limited hospitality for fear of placing a catering burden on my mother. The one great exception was a man who became a firm family friend, Alderman A.W.S. Burgess, Lord Mayor in waiting. Stan Burgess was a dedicated campaigner for the rights of man, but he and his wife had the charm and sincerity that won my mother's approval. As an adolescent I was greatly impressed with his learning and had I known the term at that time I would have called him an auto-didact. I loved his story, well worked over since then, about the docker who quizzed the Marquis of Bristol about how he had acquired his castle and lands. When the peer admitted his ancestors had fought for it, the docker offered to fight him for it. At the age of eleven or so I thought this totally encapsulated the ethos of socialism. We frequently took the Burgesses on picnic runs, drinking cider and stale cheese (all pubs had to offer in those days.) My favourite photograph shows Stan Burgess and my father in 1920's bathing suits, sitting together waist deep in muddy water at Weston-Super-Mare. Stan looking pigeon chested and thin, betraying hard working class origins; my father, the same height, but with a strong chest and muscles derived from

Dr. Datta takes a dip with Lord Mayor Stan Burgess

the regular use of his dumb bells that led my mother to refer to him as her 'pocket Hercules.'

Eventually Stan became Chairman of the Docks Committee. There is a plaque honouring his name in Avonmouth, for he was instrumental in building Bristol's celebrated Deepwater West Dock at Portishead. Civic pride was a motivating factor. In the nineteenth century Bristol had lost out (in spite of Brunel) to Liverpool and Southampton. Stan wanted to reverse the decline. He succeeded, but he was not to know the economic reality of later years. He wanted to see Bristol as a great port once more, exporting the products of British industry across the globe. But he would probably not have enjoyed seeing instead the tens of thousands of Japanese cars coming into the U.K. through Portbury Dock. It isn't quite what he, or any of us, had in mind.

In 1937 the nineteen year old daughter of my father's brother arrived to stay with us from India. She too had been under suspicion of involvement in anti-government activities, and just as in my father's case, England was a safer place to be than India. Babla, as she was named, did not settle easily in Snowdon House. She had a complex background, and possessed what my mother took to be a rather superior air. "Still waters run deep" was one of her phrases to fit the case. Nor did she offer quite the same domestic contribution that my mother might have appreciated. After a year or so she enrolled in a medical course at Bristol University and moved to a flat in Clifton. She developed close a friendship with a lady who was keenly interested in the Vedanta movement, and made many friends among the students. On a visit to the Art Gallery one day I was astonished to see her portrait in oils, done by a local artist called Cliff Brown. Later in life she married an ambitious Punjabi business man, moved to London, and began a life of some affluence. I would see much of them in the fifties. They offered a taste of good living, with pink Champagne, a fine house off Kingston Hill, and comfortable excursions by Bentley.

As a doctor at Stapleton Hospital my father's daily concern was primarily the physical well-being of seven hundred or more male and female patients. They arrived in his care from a variety of sources, including orphanages, but most were simply unable to cope with daily life for reasons of mental disability. Many were went in for long terms after some form of assessment by a local authority executive called a 'Relieving Officer'.

The term indicates his task as being a functionary of the 'Poor Law;' whose purpose was to 'relieve' the parish of unnecessary expense caused by paupers, and those deemed inadequate in some way or other. The hospital was called an Institution. It was the direct descendent of the Victorian 'Workhouse' known to sad little Oliver Twist. It represented a world of fairly ruthless measures to deal with the less fortunate. Illegitimate motherhood could lead to lifelong incarceration. A world in which there had been much injustice, long before present day welfare concerns had changed society's views of such matters. Samuel Butler's 'Erewhon' neatly summarised society's attitudes; if you fell ill you deserved to be thoroughly punished for your irresponsibility.

Certainly, in the twenties and thirties there was precious little legislation or medical training to seek any improvement in the mental capacities of those who found themselves incarcerated. My father had done his best to understand the causality that underlies the mental process of those given the Umbrella term 'insane'. or 'mentally defective'. Without being required to, he studied the writing of alleged experts in the field like Sigmund Freud and his English proselytiser, Ernest Jones. But Psychiatry as a subject barely existed. Nigel Balchin wrote a famous novel, 'Mine Own Executioner' on the lack of acceptance by the medical establishment of psycho-somatic explanation.

A Diploma in Psychiatric Medicine was instituted and my father went to London and took the first part, but war intervened to cut short his completion of the qualification. In any case, the studies of Freud seemed to apply overwhelming to the problems of often well-heeled middle class Viennese. In general it was the inadequacy of social provision for, and scientific analysis of, those in his care that confirmed my father's dedication to socialist principles. The First World War had put the social aspect of the problem into perspective. If officers like Siegfried Sassoon or Wilfred Owen cracked under the strains of warfare, they were sent for therapy (as documented by Pat Barker) to a rest home like Craiglockhart.

If a private soldier gave in to shell shock, he was likely to be shot at dawn.

The only hope for mental institutions seemed to lie with the election of a Labour Government and against this frequently grim background my father contrived to counteract the physical ills of his many patients, with a dispensary to provide such treatments as were known to general practice. Frequently too, he had to carry out Post Mortems, and attend Coroners Inquests; occasions for some trepidation since Coroners knew both Medicine and Law, and he himself carried total responsibility.

The diversity of his patients is reflected in two of his favourite anecdotes. On one occasion a man who was brought in for assessment took one look at him, shouted "You are God!" and struck him full in the face. 'A fine way to treat the Deity' was my father's rueful comment. His favourite case brought him at least some way closer to the rarified postulates of Sigmund Freud. A navvy was suffering total paralysis of the right arm after an accident with a pickaxe. My father spent much time talking to this otherwise healthy labourer, who seemed otherwise perfectly 'compos mentis'. After prolonged questioning, he found out that the man's wife had sued for divorce, but still required alimony payments. It then transpired that she was living with his marital successor. My father contacted a solicitor, arranged a meeting, a court hearing, and eventually the man was relieved of his alimony demand. Three months later came a knock on the door. His patient grabbed my father's hand and pumped it with his 'paralysed' arm, declaring - 'I owe you so much Doctor. You've cured my poor old arm completely. I'm back at work now.'

If such a case of 'hysterical paralysis' validates Freud's work on the unconscious, perhaps he cannot be totally written off as the modern equivalent of a witch doctor.

Chapter 7

My friendship with the Master's son was short lived but sincere. Frank had amazingly blond hair, blue eyes and an engaging smile like Mickey Rooney. We raced around on juvenile bicycles and both had Hornby electric train sets, Christmas presents from devoted parents. We lived in G.W.R. country and the only model Hornby made was a somewhat dated 'County Class' 4-4-0. Frank's father came from the Midlands so his had to be from that glamorous L.M.S. 4-6-2 range, named after Duchesses and Princesses. They were longer, had more complex driving gear, and of course were in L.M.S. red. But I learned to live with it.

Another youngster joined us and assisted our tentative efforts to play cricket on the handkerchief sized area of grass that lay between our house and the hospital. His name was Ernie Edgar, and he did not have a train set. He lived in a little cottage down the hill and he was nearly two years older. His father had taken a German bullet near the heart on the Somme, but was able to work at the bus station.

Ernie had leadership qualities. He took the cricket bat and showed how to hit a six over the wall of a deserted nearby house called "The Grange". Unfortunately that meant the ball was lost because the house was too "spooky" for any of us to climb over and look for it. Soon after that Frank's father characteristically withdrew the use of the cricket gear. Ernie's enterprise came to the fore once more when we discovered a newly invented game called "Monopoly". It was Frank who had access to the set and we settled down to figure it out in my father's study. We had enjoyed a week or so of Monopoly when again Frank's father struck. Use of the set was withdrawn. So Ernie took charge. He ordered me to provide paper, coloured crayons and scissors. Then, under his command we sat down and began to make our own Monopoly set. We never finished it of course, but the Edgar leadership was proved. Not for nothing was his family named after the ancestor Alfred, the greatest King of Wessex.

Next came the all important matter of bicycles. For many

months a local shop had given a proud window display to a wonderful machine called a "Dawes". Drop handlebars, "derailleur" 3 speed, cable brakes, celluloid mudguards, the full "equipe racing" spec. Above all it had thrilling chromium plated front forks. It was priced at more than eight pounds, and Ernie, who had to walk two miles every day to get to his school, decided he was going to own it. He delivered greengroceries, and even went to work for Gerald. Gerald Taylor had inherited his father's small factory, which made inks and gravy browning. He lived in a fine Victorian house, with the factory tucked away at the back. Most said that the liquids he made was the same stuff in different bottles. He was well known locally by his nickname "Inky", and he lived with his sister, a very stylish lady who had a little baby, but no husband. Sadly "Inky had long since turned alcoholic, mainly through the proximity of our local "The Old Tavern". His product used hundreds of bottles which had to be washed and labelled. So Ernie joined the workforce. It was sporadic employment because Inky only made enough product to be able to go on another "bender", which he did by driving his Rolls Royce Phantom into town until apprehended by the constabulary, who had to pedal quite fast to catch him.

At long last Ernie counted his savings, walked to the cycle shop and placed eight pounds, twelve shillings and sixpence on the counter, saying;

'Mr. Gibbs, please, I'd like to have that Dawes you have in your window.'

He became the cycling trend setter of the entire neighbourhood, cleaning and oiling it when not showing us how to ride. His stock was Everest high. But within a year he was not alone. I and a friend simply had to join him as Dawes owners with chromium front forks. The difference was devoted parents paid for ours.

Adolescents gather in large groups and nowadays strike fear into local residents. We also foregathered, but we intimidated no-one because we had a rather special rallying point. This was a little old house cum sweetshop in Manor Road, near to Hannah More's birthplace. It was run by a woman called Lil Wilcox and her 'Gran'. She was tolerant, quick witted and entertaining. We teased, and she teased back. War fever was growing, and on one memorable occasion she took her Bible and pointed out the "number of the Beast", 666 in the book of Revelations. She then proceeded to translate it into letters which spelt "ADOLF HITLER".

I was hugely impressed, and indeed remain so. I was never able to do it myself. When war came Lil made it her business to nominate any potential fifth columnists in the neighbourhood, who might be leaving lights on for the enemy to see. She also organised the collection of milk bottle tops to make Spitfires and we were able to contribute most of the cost of a new "City and Marine" ambulance.

When one hears Public School boys complain about the awfulness of their lives, they are surely lamenting the absence of family and friends enjoyed by those of us who came home at four o'clock, and had fun, sometimes even getting to know girls. Frank's father though, gave him no such concessions, and he was sent to Taunton, and later to Millfield, the most expensive boarding school around.

On Sundays we took a little more care over our appearance and went for walks in Snuff Mills. Never to Church though; Sunday was a day when it might be possible to meet up with girls, the initiative being taken by Ernie and another older friend of his, Alan. To this end we did the most extraordinary things to our hair. We plastered it with the most objectionable forms of grease and oil, one of which was called Brylcreem. This was a white adhesive that came in a stumpy jar and was advertised everywhere by England's most famous cricketer, Denis Compton. We massaged it into our hair, and ran combs through it frequently in an effort to achieve the precise effect of waves breaking on the sea shore. It was a horrible performance and in Summer, after much patting, well lubricated flakes of dandruff mingled with the sweat and ran down faces on to collars. When war came the advertising icon became an airman in uniform, and those who joined the R.A.F. were called "The Brylcreem Boys".

At the height of the War, Ernie, who was a Sea Cadet, learned of a special scheme which offered a fast route, whereby suitable candidates might become Naval Officers. Aged seventeen and a half, he volunteered, and after exhaustive tests and a selection board, was enrolled as likely material. Called up at eighteen he successfully completed the full range of training and duties, and was awarded a commission just before his nineteenth birthday. Only in wartime did the Royal Navy award such a qualification to boys born in cottages. In October 1944 he sailed in a convoy of various ships including Vosper Motor Gunboats, and a flotilla of Fairmile Bs. In one of these, as Sub Lieutenant Ernest Edgar, he was appointed as watchkeeping Officer, with attendant navigational duties, en route from Milford Haven to Gibraltar After a long voyage through the Med. with many ports of call, including Suez, the Persian Gulf, and the coast of India, the flotilla sailed into Rangoon, to become a "clean up" force operating along the "Chaungs" of Southern Burma.

* * *

At age ten or so I had been sent for the best education affordable to Bristol Grammar School Preparatory School. It was a whole new world of experience, coupled with a little learning, that would dominate life for the next eight years and beyond. My Form Master was a Scot named MacGregor, who had taught my brother twelve years before. He was a pure gem of a teacher, a writer of boy's books, and he planted values deep. He loved choral singing and battled with our thin, off-key, breathless voices to try and inculcate some appreciation of the vox humana. It was he, as long ago as that, who insisted that we listen to the Festival of Nine Lessons and Carols from King's College at Christmas.

No one should doubt the opportunities for mental advancement given at such a school by so many gifted and dedicated teachers. The fact that so many of their charges would fail to benefit from them, with little urge to read a book, can never be laid at their door.

There was one glittering exception at least to this defeatist rule.

He was a boy possessed of much nervous energy who kept nagging teachers to do what he called "putting on a show" at the end of the year. So 'Mackie' gave him the stage, and he recruited me into the cast. He said that his father was an 'entertainer' who went to Army camps and such places, and performed what he called "scripts". He persuaded me to deliver one of these. It consisted of pretending to be an angry tenant sitting at a telephone and complaining that the wind had blown down his shutters. ("No, not shut up-shutters!") With my advanced years and experience the script seemed to me not very funny, so I decided to re-write it. The result was a disaster. Nobody laughed, and I crawled off the stage. I had learned the only lesson I needed to learn about the difference between real talent and wishful thinking.

More than forty years on (as playwrights say) I was invited by a female friend to see a new play that was much talked about at the Apollo Theatre, Shaftesbury Avenue. It was called 'Down Forget me not Lane'. The curtain was not long up before some of the ideas began to have a familiar ring. The writer was reminiscing about his father, an entertainer who used to put on shows at local army camps. I seized the programme and squinted in the half light at the author's details. His name was Peter Nichols, and he was my Prep. school chum. I watched the rest of the show in a glow of nostalgic inebriation.

But there was more to come. Nichols had another play on at the London Old Vic called 'The National Health'. Its black humour was a send up of all the TV medical soap operas of the day. It seemed the country's whole medical establishment was flocking to see it. The Old Vic could not afford to take it off, and was in danger of becoming a repertory theatre.

'A Day in the Death of Joe Egg' was his ultimate triumph, revived many times after, and made into an Oscar-deserving film starring Alan Bates. Perhaps a final irony is that even Peter Nichols had a part to play in the closure of the British Empire. As a school leaver he had been conscripted into the army and posted to Malaya to fight against what were known as 'communist bandits'. The Film

"Privates on Parade" was his memory of those years.

Another significant boy joined school at the same time. From Dr. Bell's came ruggedly fit Austin Davis, he of the mother's white shoes. He had won the first of several scholarships and before long was being selected and groomed for a pure classical education. Austin also lived in Fishponds, and occasionally joined our little gatherings, but as often as not was seen carrying his music case to his piano teacher, a talent he fostered throughout his life. And lest this image be taken to imply some kind of ultra-sensitive nature, one must record that he won his weight at the school boxing contest, became an excellent rugby fullback for Oxford, was a better swimmer than any of us, and eventually won a "Blue" at water polo.

One might see him as a Renaissance Man in the making who would, in time, develop several more Florentine characteristics, of Lombard Street inclination.

After a year or so in the "Prep" I graduated to the Main School and was at once overwhelmed by the tradition inherent in a 400 year old Grammar School. To a ten year old the Great Hall was an awe inspiring cathedral of a place, with a lofty hammer beam roof, oak panelling on all sides, accessed by a double stone staircase that passed under the organ loft. It was built in the 1870's of Avon Gorge red stone, and had a fine clock and bell tower with flagpole. Benches were grouped around ten impressive teachers' 'thrones' of solid oak, from which the learned gentlemen held forth to properly respectful students. The noise must nevertheless have been considerable and by the turn of the century 'normal' classrooms were instituted on other floors.

But in addition to its architectural grandeur, the school boasted one exceptional feature that few of its rivals could hope to equal; the Bristol Grammar School School Song. No mere 'song' indeed, but a positive anthem that could compare with anything heard in Westminster Abbey at any time of national rejoicing. The words were naturally enough entirely in Latin, having been composed by a celebrated Old Harrovian educationalist, called Sir Cyril Norwood, who held court at Bristol between 1905 and 1916. The music was by a composer called Stear, inspired beyond doubt by Purcell and Handel in equal measure. It began with four mighty descending chords, repeated to lead in to the first joyously trumpeted line;

"Nunc Universo Gaudio
Ludo Pensisque functi..."

Major chords followed on, rising up the scale to a triumphant shout,

"Concelebremus Cuncti"

Then, as if emotions had not been adrenalised enough there came a colossal War Cry of a chorus;

"Sit clarior, sit dignior
Quotquot labuntur menses
Sit primus nobis hic decor :
Sumus BRISTOLIENSES"

On the final chorus it was customary to lift the last syllable by an entire octave, which produced something like a scream of tribal civic pride, worthy of a gathering of King Cetawayo's most feared assegai wielding warriors.

For all of this the "backing" was the school organ, played "fortissimo", until the ears recoiled. I have heard many school songs, but mere songs are what they are, even if, as at Raynes Park, written by W.H.Auden. They fade into oblivion when compared with this magnum opus of Norwood and Stear. It is possible to go almost anywhere in the world and wherever two or more Old Bristolians are gathered together, all one has to do is produce the opening introductory descending chords of "Boom, Boom, Boom, Boom" to produce a whole oratorio of a performance for those present. It may be the only Latin they ever learned, but they will carry it with them till they draw their last breaths.

***

No picture of an idyllic childhood in England can be complete without an allusion to a four footed friend. Mine was called Roy. A man who ran a local paper shop had ordered him, none too cleverly from a labrador breeder in Scotland. When the animal took a long time to arrive he lost patience and bought an Airedale locally. The result was a period when he lived in a small flat, with two big hound dogs tearing it to pieces to get at each other. Distraught he came to my father (always known as a soft touch) and I thus acquired this animal, worthy of a Disney film script. He was somewhat taller than most labradors, and had a shaggy coat. I came to suspect a touch of wolf hound in his ancestry; but he loved water, swam regularly across the Frome, and was only outclassed by a local Jack Russell who could actually dive off a bridge. His name puzzled some people, and having had a teacher called MacGregor, I explained that he must originally have been called Rob Roy, one of that clan's heroes, but well known as a rustler.

It was entirely legitimate for me to have an air rifle, and I acquired a very powerful Webley. I acted as a voluntary hunter attacking the large flock of rooks which came to strip the cherry trees. Roy was an enthusiastic gun dog, but had to be discouraged from eating the dead birds which the head gardener hung in the trees as a dire warning. I noticed in due course that the rooks no longer came in a flock, but sent out pairs of scouts to see if we were lying in wait.

Roy was wonderful with people, but he had an unfortunate deep rooted streak of delinquency, presumably brought on by his unhappy puppy time experiences; he would attack other animals, and more than once, I had to stop him from finishing off someone's Alsatian. However he never laid a tooth on any biped.

Four legs bad, two legs good was his motto.

Chapter 8

My father was not the first Indian to come to Bristol motivated by reforming zeal. A hundred years previously a most remarkable Bengali called Raja Rammohan Roy had visited Stapleton in fact, and stayed with a Unitarian family called the Carpenters. Roy was an energetic reformer possessed of a formidable intellect, who had studied Sanskrit, Persian, Arabic, Hebrew and Greek. He had achieved a senior post in the government of Bengal, in a country now wholly controlled by the East India Company. In a newly founded college he campaigned hard for the introduction of European rather than traditional Hindu studies He opposed idol worship and the traditional suicide of widows on husbands' funeral pyres.

Roy came to England to pursue his reforms with the Privy Council, and also to ask for an increase in the stipend of the titular Mogul Emperor, who was a vassal of the Company . However it was his progressive religious ideas that caught the attention of many English intellectuals, including the Carpenters. The movement he had started was called the "Brahmo Somaj "and in essence he had distilled all the aspects of monotheism to be found in the Hindu scriptures. My great grandfather had been one of his keenest followers, and this had led to a family rift. His monotheism was also allied to criticism of the multiple nature of the Deity as in Christian belief, and it was this that gave him such an appeal to Unitarians in Britain, ultimately leading to the Theosophical movement.

In his short stay in England Roy made a great impact, and was invited to attend the coronation of William1V. He preached at Lewin's Mead Chapel in Bristol, and a magnificent full length portrait of him was commissioned which hangs in the City Art Gallery.

But Bristol was not kind to Roy. After only a few days, he contracted meningitis and died. A striking memorial in Hindu style was built for him by the Tagore family in Arno's Vale cemetery His death has been commemorated every year since by a delegation from India House, and my father played host to them in later years

After one Mutiny, and a century of struggle, my father had grown to believe that India could only win its independence if a Labour government were elected in Britain, and he devoted his energies to that end. Gandhi and the Congress party were treated with total contempt by Winston Churchill, who called the apostle of non violence a "naked fakir", and recorded his view of Indians as being as undesirable as the Germans. Living in England also made one conscious of the power of the concept of Empire and from this standpoint, Gandhi's various protest marches, "fasts unto death", and even his famous visits to Lancashire and the East End could at times seem like futile gestures with no real effect on the seat of Conservative power in Westminister.

Constitutional reforms had been made in Queen Victoria's time and by the Morley-Minto reforms of 1909, but the most the British would ever consider was 'Dominion Status' and this was emphatically rejected when Nehru declared 'Independence Day' in 1930, and Gandhi began his famous 'salt march' to the sea. This signalled the start of the 'Civil Disobedience Campaign' which involved breaking all British made laws and boycotting British goods.

Throughout the thirties the story was one of 'Round Table' conferences, withdrawal of Congress participation, imprisonment of leaders, occasional outbreaks of violence, and a repetition of this pattern up to the outbreak of war. There was a mutiny in the Indian Navy, and Subhas Bose went over to the Japanese, forming a "Free India " force to fight with them against the British.

My father's contribution was to introduce the subject of Indian Independence at Labour party meetings whenever possible and give talks to all kinds of organisations in support of Congress Party tactics. For him in England there was no question of illegality, but problems of a different kind arose for someone who was also pursuing a professional career. He told of a moment when one member of his audience stood up and shouted "You dirty Bengali soor!" at him before storming out. He recounts this incident wryly as being greatly impressed that an English person in the audience would even know the Bengali word for "pig".

Perhaps more painful was a debate at the University, when his motion for Indian Independence was opposed with some vigour and effectiveness by a certain professor of Imperial History called MacInnes, the father of a school friend of mine, who had a whole Institute in the City to foster his views. The audience was heavily biased in favour of the eminent gentleman whose views were truly those of Churchill, who said that "sooner or later we shall have to crush Gandhi and the Congress."

The first Indian ever to make an impact on the British political scene had been Saklatvala, a member of the Tata family of wealthy industrialists who nevertheless joined the Communist Party, and after years of campaigning for wage increases was elected to Parliament in 1922 for Battersea. His popularity with his British working class electors was extraordinary, and he was arrested for his speeches during the General Strike. He was constantly under surveillance, and utterly hated by all who loved the Empire. But as a campaigner for industrialisation he also took issue with Gandhi, and as a member of the Communist Party he could not join the main Labour leadership, though he earned Attlee's respect.

Saklatvala's mantle was taken over by an equally remarkable man called Krishna Menon, who came to England in 1924 and began a career in publishing, helping Alan Lane (famous old boy of Bristol Grammar School) to found Penguin and Pelican books.

Menon was a tall, gaunt dynamo of a man, almost twitching with nervous energy. He had deep set eyes, collar length grey hair, and a hawk nose that suggested a Peregrine diving on its prey He was a South Indian, descended from a royal line of Kerala, and his intellectual capacity was phenomenal. He collected first degrees in literature and science, and Masters'degrees in psychology and political theory, before being called to the bar at the Middle Temple. At L.S.E. he came under the influence of Harold Laski, and thereafter remained a dedicated socialist. In 1932 he became a St' Pancras Councillor, alongside Barbara Castle, and combined work for the under privileged with a career in publishing. He was literary editor of the Bodley Head, which Sir Alan Lane inherited from his uncle, and used as a springboard to found Penguin Books. Menon brought his experience of the 20th Century Library to become General Editor of Pelican books, a division of Penguin with an educational bias.

One can well imagine that his fiery brilliance was inimical to the genteel Allen Lane, and a rift was inevitable. But his name remains as general editor of Pelican books from its foundation, and his list of thirty titles became required reading for a whole generation. It included G.D.H. Cole on economics, Tawney's "Religion and the Rise of Capitalism" Freud's "Psychopathology of Everyday Life," and Clive Bell's "Civilisation", books which brought the thinking of great minds within reach of millions.

The break with Lane left Menon free to devote himself to the India League and Indian Independence He won the support of intellectuals like Bertrand Russell, J.B.S. Haldane, and dozens of Labour Party activists such as Fenner Brockway, Reverend Sorensen Ian Mikardo, Ellen Wilkinson, Bevin and Attlee. He published News India, and wrote innumerable pamphlets and articles in media newspapers and the New Statesman. He spoke regularly at Hyde Park, and in every major British city.

Like so many others my father became his devoted admirer, and those aspects of Menon's character which some found fearsome, simply won my father's affection. As a Bengali he found much to admire in South Indians; they came from a thousand miles away from his home and spoke an utterly different language but they still had this mysterious perspective that made them "Indians", He particularly admired their flair for mathematics, and Menon's intellectual versatility was no surprise to him.

"Such brilliant mathematicians, South Indians" he used to remark. My mother on the other hand was most concerned for his physical survival. It was well known that he slept only briefly and lived on innumerable cups of tea and currant buns. When he stayed with us she made sure he had some "square" (though still vegetarian) meals, and she darned his socks. "The poor man needs a wife" was her constant refrain; but no such need ever seemed to enter Menon's daunting work schedule.

Under his influence my father made several trips to London to speak at meetings and on more than one occasion at 'Speakers Corner' in Hyde Park. The philosophy of Gandhism; - non-violence, home-spinning, anti-industrialism, romantic asceticism was something I never heard my father comment upon. As a Marxist, and presumed believer in revolution he had adopted views that came out of the industrially intense and embattled world as analysed by Marx, Engels, Lenin and Trotsky. Gandhi seemed to hark back to an earlier epoch of Rousseau, Ruskin, Wordsworth, William Morris. He had read them all and found them enjoyable but irrelevant.

Born a Hindu he enjoyed his Sunday Roast with horseradish sauce as much as any middle class Englishman. He relished all the pleasures his adopted country had to offer; comedy and variety shows on the radio as well as Shakespeare and Milton. But he longed for fairer societies throughout the world. Like Krishna Menon and Saklatvala before him he had strong 'fellow travelling' sympathies, which were entirely legitimate during the war when we all admired the bravery and self-sacrifice of Stalin's Russia.

On the other hand it was Gandhism that would eventually capture the admiration of sensitive, ethically responsive, politically conscious sections of the West, and it seemed to many observers that the massive movement he led, would overwhelm British Imperialism by sheer weight of moral rectitude. It was the romance of Gandhism that the film-makers found irresistible, and genuine Christians felt he belonged in the New Testament rather than to a purely political movement.

Nonetheless there is one nagging element in the debate that causes a certain discomfort. Gandhi could triumph because there was a whole background of English moral thinking from minds such as Locke, Mill, Bentham, Wilberforce and others, which made the British Empire look like a disgraceful contradiction of all that every thinking Englishman held dear. Gandhi made the English look like hypocrites. In the long run they had to forget Churchill and give up the Empire.

And one nagging question offers itself at once. If Nazi Germany had ruled India, where then would the Mahatma have been?

Meanwhile, the Indian nationalists who campaigned in Britain for Indian Independence had a simple practicality about their approach. India had a been governed from London since the days of the East India Company. Only a radical change of government in Westminister could bring about the legal changes necessary to achieve Independence. It was this above all that led people like Saklatvala, Menon, my father, and many others to direct their energies in the way that they did.

Without their efforts there might well have been no Mountbattens, no Stafford Cripps, and no 1944 vital Labour Party Conference at which my father was a delegate and leading speaker. and which gave the Labour government instructions to free India as soon as it was elected.

***

Imperialism was by no means an exclusively British phenomenon. In the thirties, two other leading European nations embarked on policies of conquest which would eventually bring the whole world to the abyss. In Italy, Mussolini and his Fascist party aped his imagined Roman forbears by invading North Africa and occupying Abyssinia. Even more disastrous were the racial theories of the German Nazi party which led Hitler on his insane attempt to subjugate or remove the allegedly "inferior" races within his own borders and in Europe at large.

The rehersal theatre for these vile extravagances proved to be Spain, and when the Fascist Caudillo set out to destroy the left wing government there, Civil War ensued. To the great mass of self-satisfied middle England, such matters were the concerns of foreigners, who belonged, in Chamberlains famous words, to "far off countries of which we know little." However, thinkers, especially on the British left, saw exactly what was happening and the bravest of them went to join the International Brigade. They included a teacher from my school called Chris Shipham who would in due course endeavour to teach me Spanish, and help me become one of the first to take the language for Bristol Higher Certificate, and for which a special exam had to be set by the University.

Had my father been 25 years younger and single, he would no doubt have joined them; but his "Galsworthy's Winchester" days were over. Spain allowed Hitler and Goering to try out their Junkers and Heinkel bombers on a little Basque town called "Guernica", which inspired the most famous black and white painting of all time. Only political sophisticates in England realised what Spain was about. When Laurie Lee set out to walk there "one Midsummer morning", he soon turned back when the shooting started. Even a left wing sympathiser like George Orwell used Catalonia to indulge what some would call a certain misanthropy in his writing.

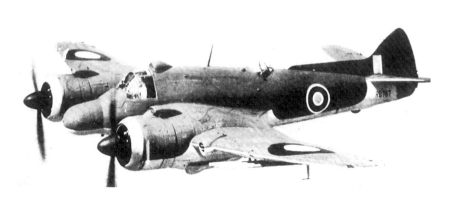

The Bristol Beaufighter Mark X

Chapter 9

The idea that the whole world would soon be convulsed in a terrible war filtered only slowly into the brain of a pre-teenage boy. Life was unquestionably sweet, all kinds of pleasures and adventures abounded. Parents were indulgent, a bar of chocolate was a mere twopence, summer evenings were long and the Wall's Ice-cream man pedalled up Snowdon Road every day. In school, dedicated teachers coaxed one's mind into an understanding of the weirdness of Latin, the stresses of mathematics. One was delighted to find that even the fearsome Shakespeare might contain, as in 'Macbeth', adventures as good as those in one's own comics like Hotspur and Rover.

One was also introduced to the pleasure of Rugby football, an activity that would form quite a significant (if mindless) role in one's development. To discover that one could catch the ball, swerve round an opponent and perhaps even score a try was a most satisfying experience.

For my brother Albion, much older than I, Rugby was a serious matter. He studied medicine at Bristol University and played regularly for their team, occasionally being chosen to play for Bristol. My father was immensely proud of his six foot son's athletic prowess, and we often went to Coombe Dingle to watch him play. I was much impressed by the manners of the supporters, who always addressed my father as "Sir", and by the cafeteria which offered tea with cream slices and Battenberg cake.

In that cosy, easy, sunlit world of the late thirties, the notion that the skies over England could be filled with bombers raining death was more like a fantasy from H.G. Wells than a real possibility.

My father would have known precisely what was happening in Germany, with its Reichstag fire trials and Nuremberg rallies, but to ordinary people in England, Germany conjured up a picture of open air living, camping and mountaineering, a really rather desirable lifestyle. The only odd thing was German stamps which had quite crazy values like 'one million Deutschemarks.' Very hard to explain that. I recall my brother even singing a German song "Bei mir bist du schoen". It was only many years late that one realised this was not so much German as Yiddish, and herein lay a distinction that would lead to years of future horror.

In the months leading up to Munich, my father continued to divide his life 'in tres partes' between politics, his family and his medical work. Much of the latter was routine medical practice, limited by the simple remedies of the day without penicillin or mood altering drugs. He had to perform 'post mortems' too, and usually felt apprehensive at the critical questioning delivered by Coroners, who combined sound medical knowledge with wide legal experience. In the absence of structured research into mental illness, he learned what he could by observation and common sense. His medical studies also led to the secret presence of another member of the household. He or she occupied a box in a deep cupboard in the study and was simply known as 'The Skeleton'. As a child I always cast nervous glances in that direction when entering the room. Growing up, it led to a whole complex of philosophical ruminations on the matter of life and death. "Alas poor Yorick" was Shakespeare's great contribution to the subject; I too found myself worrying about his or her origins; who my father might have bought it from, whether it was right to talk about 'owning' it (clearly there could only be one true owner; the person who was born with it.) Had the owner given consent to be sold? In what country did it originate? Was it a sinister case of grave robbing?

In later life I grew less sensitive on the subject and was not above using it when making a TV commercial about Wookey Hole Caves. And I was quite relieved when an antique dealer in Bath disposed of it to a free spending tourist from Texas.

Perhaps in anticipation of the dark days to come, my father decided on the most memorable holiday of all; to the Scottish Highlands. In days before Motorways the journey to our intended base in Oban would take four days, and be a severe test of the Riley's dependability. In the event the whole adventure was a triumph. From our boarding house on the front we skirted lochs celebrated in song, took ferries like Ballachulish and Loch Etive, passed through the glowering pass of Glencoe, gazed on the majesty of Ben Nevis. We took a Caledonian steamer to Mull, walked on the strange stones of Staffa, looked respectfully at St. Columba's chapel on Iona. We walked through heather steps, smelt the tangle of the Isles, and on one occasion my father borrowed a dinghy and rowed me to the Island of Kerrera humming "speed bonny boat" all the way.

When we finally returned to Bristol we disgorged loads of presents, most of mine rather naturally bearing the MacGregor tartan, and my mother proudly showed how her long shepherd's crook served perfectly to draw the heavy curtains in Snowdon House.If there was an apotheosis of a charmed childhood this must be it, for I never met another boy in Bristol who had journeyed so far.

***

A year later, in a choked voice, Chamberlain announced that we were at war with Germany.

Adolescents are so self-obsessed that even the prospect of death and destruction fails to fill them with the apprehension felt by adults like my mother. She knew her son would 'have to go'. Perhaps even both of us.

For the moment though we were lead to what someone has erroneously called the "Phoney War". This manifested itself with much amusement in the issue of gas masks, which were put on in school and provided a welcome break from studying the coalfields of Britain; when one breathed out heavily, they produced an irresistible farting noise. The filling of sandbags became a national occupation as though we were preparing to shoot invading Germans from all directions. Sticky tape was plastered over windows, and blackout material began to arrive for screening them. Car headlights were given little masks and night driving became quite dangerous. Anderson shelters were distributed to most homes and in our case, men arrived from the hospital to dig a deep hole in my mother's back lawn, and erect a two foot thick concrete shelter with bunk beds.

Aerial activity increased quite noticeably and slow moving training planes, bombers and bi-planes roared overhead giving us confidence. But it was a long time before anyone saw a Spitfire. At school too, shelters were built and air-raid precautions practised. The one activity which gained a new impetus was the 'Officer's Training Corps' which drilled and marched behind our rather impressive brass band led by a drum major, complete with silver crowned mace, which he could throw high into the air and catch with death defying precision. Once a year a 'Field Day' was held when the Corps marched out to engage in the pretence of attacking and defending their chosen position. If the route lay across the Clifton Suspension Bridge, the order was given to "break step"; old army hands knew that if this was not done it might start the bridge swaying and Isambard Kingdom Brunel's masterpiece would plunge two hundred feet into the Avon Gorge, taking with it the flower of Bristol's military youth. Apart from that, nobody knew much about what was happening in the manoeuvres; which therefore made it a perfect representation of real conflict, normally enveloped in the "fog of war."

Rationing was brought in quite early on, with two eggs per month per person, and so was Conscription although it seemed an easy matter to obtain deferment. As in the earlier World War, a British Expeditionary Force, ill-equipped and poorly trained, was sent to France and British concern for the Empire ensured that equal numbers of troops, supported by men from the Dominions and Colonies, were sent to North Africa and Malaysia to guard Imperial life-lines like the Suez Canal, and (most optimistic of all), Singapore.

At home, at least the Churchill- led government recognised the seriousness of the threat posed by the Wehrmacht, and a part-time force of old soldiers and young patriots was mustered to be known as 'Local Defence Volunteers'. Weapons and ammunition were almost non- existent and when bayonets were fastened to broom handles in lieu, wiseacres in Parliament made speeches extolling the virtues of the Pike in British battles again French Cavalry. The force was soon more sensibly renamed the Home Guard, and although it found an immortal place as 'Dad's Army' in later British Television, it was in deadly earnest at the time, and even included trained suicide squads.

My childhood adulation of the Royal Navy soon received a set-back of a personal kind that put the whole matter of war into perspective. My brother's fiancee was one of three attractive sisters and we usually spent alternate Christmases with their parents, the Brain family. One day a memorable young man was met, a boyfriend of one of the girls. No-one could fail to find him attractive, a handsome fair-haired young midshipman for whom the song 'the sailor with the navy blue eyes' might have been written. Such was his charm that he even took notice of me, and quietly gave me a sixpence, an act of unforgettable generosity to one of my age. Soon he left to join his ship, an aircraft carrier called H.M.S. Courageous. No-one would be surprised to learn that the first blow in the war at sea was struck by the Germans. A German U-boat torpedoed and sank the 'Courageous' within weeks of war being declared. Of the 1,500 crew, nearly half were drowned. My benefactor was one of them. Hitler personally congratulated the Captain of the submarine on getting the war off to a good start, and there would be much more of the kind to come.

Perhaps our years of gladness subtly became affected when shops began to put up notices reading 'no chocolates, no sweets.' We knew we too had to take things seriously.

There was beyond the River Frome a low hill known as Purdown. Military activity on it soon revealed that gun emplacements were being built; at the same time elephantine 'Barrage Balloons' began to raise their flapping ears from parks all over the city.

Then one day the four anti-aircraft guns fired some practice rounds. The noise was utterly deafening. Even Snowdon House, with its thick stone walls shook. Rumours spread around Fishponds that there was "a sixteen inch" naval gun on Purdown. In fact it was simply that the guns were linked to fire in pairs, but for all that our morale was raised by their shattering roar.

Which of course was precisely what Churchill intended when he gave priority to the installation of anti-aircraft guns in all British cities. He made many mistakes, but he knew what bombing could do to morale, and he wisely made sure that the sound and fury of British guns, whether they hit anything or not, would show that we could fight back, and re-build confidence in urban populations.

Beyond Purdown lay the Bristol Aeroplane Company, producer of many successful aircraft and air-cooled radial engines. The most thrilling sight and sound of all was that of a new twin-engined silver fighter plane being put through its paces. It seemed to streak vertically upwards into the heavens, engines screaming, then turned over and plunged vertically downwards at colossal speeds that almost guaranteed the pilot's death. The plane was called the Bristol Beaufighter, and day after day I watched in awestruck excitement as the Test pilot took it close to destruction. Soon this exciting plane would be in service, as an effective night fighter and torpedo bomber. Perhaps it never achieved the glamour of the Spitfire, but its versatility was immense and it was in action in every war zone. The 'Beaufighter' was one of my city's great war achievements and, I found myself switching adulation to the R.A.F., leaving the Royal Navy to take care of itself.

***

With the British Empire in serious jeopardy, it might be thought that those committed to independence for India and the colonies would be quick to take advantage of the situation. However until the Japanese took Singapore, and a man called Bose founded the Indian National Army, this was certainly not so; indeed among Indians living in Britain the very opposite was often the case.

My father joined the St. John's Ambulance Brigade, and began to teach First Aid, something he kept up two or three times a week for six years. In London the fiery Krishna Menon became one of the first Air Raid Wardens, charged with keeping the blackout and helping to cope with bomb damage. Both men however would have

Wartime service as an officer with St. Johns
(Photo courtesy of Bristol United Press)

had certain problems of a political nature. If as true Socialists they believed that this war was the ultimate showdown between the forces of Fascist Imperialism and the liberation of the Proletariat, Joseph Stalin complicated matters. In August 1939 he and Adolf Hitler signed a non aggression pact which allowed them to divide Poland between them. The pact was far from the dreams of Trotsky's World revolution and it had to be rationalised very fast indeed within the pages of the Daily Worker, and other organs of the far left. Harry Pollitt of the Communist Party had to resign, in favour of Palme Dutt. The only answer was to trust Uncle Joe's wise judgement in buying time to prepare for the Nazi's inevitable attack. He also had to invade Finland with that in mind. and at least it would mean that the Germans would have to cover the whole of Eastern Poland before they could set foot on Russian soil.

Only when "Barbarossa" finally came about in 1940 could left wingers voice their support for the rectitude and courage of the Soviet Socialist Republics.

During this period my brother married his childhood sweetheart Peggy, in a typically unannounced manner. They came to live with us in Snowdon House. Peggy was a Domestic Science teacher, and an excellent cook. Gradually my mother yielded pride of place to her in the kitchen and my father responded warmly to her culinary skills; her apple crumbles were unforgettable, and every teatime witnessed the demolition of huge platefuls of tomato and cucumber sandwiches. Her daughter Anne was borne shortly before my brother was called upon for service in the Royal Army Medical Corps.

As a dedicated cowboy my main interest was in handling his Service revolver, a Smith and Wesson .38.

Chapter 10

The first inkling of a night time air raid was my mother's voice gently breaking into midnight dreams, saying;

'Wake up, David, wake up. It's an air raid, but its nothing to worry about. We all have to go to the shelter'.

The shelter was cold, damp and cramped. After an hour or so little seemed to be happening above ground or in the air, and when the 'all clear' sounded we were glad to make our exit. The process was repeated several times in the weeks that followed, and we soon felt the shelter could be dispensed with. My brother had by then qualified as a doctor and he spent many of his 'intern' nights at the General Hospital. Close to Temple Meads station it received its share of incendiary bombs which he and his colleagues threw sand over, and tried to cover with metal dustbin lids. If there were casualties he didn't mention them.

Then in the autumn of 1940 Goering decided that the Port of Bristol, with its supply lines to America, must be neutralised. Up to sixty Heinkels and Dorniers came in waves. The sky was lit by great waving search-lights and anti-aircraft guns thundered their defiance. Bombs fell with a screaming noise and soon the centre of Bristol began to glow red.

Memories of the many heavy raids during the next year tend to blur into one another, with a few burnished images standing out. Because we lived six miles from the centre of the city we felt less vulnerable. The bombers seemed to pass over us, releasing their bombs a few seconds later. But the gunfire was all pervasive, with shattering blasts on all sides. Necklaces of tracer bullets, surprisingly slow-moving, streamed skywards. I became conscious of a somewhat reprehensible change of attitude; instead of fear, excitement set in. Brought up on films of cowboys loosing off their six guns, here I was in the middle of a far greater din than ever Tom Mix could have conjured up. And this was for real. There were people up there actually trying to kill me; although in fact there was more to fear from shell splinters pattering down than actual bombs. On one occasion I poked my head out of the kitchen doorway and something thudded into the earth beside me. It was the nose cone of an anti aircraft shell, complete with fuse markings and weighed enough to have gone right through me.

We also learned that you don't hear the bomb that is going to kill you. Far off, the screaming sound is frighteningly clear. Close by it is more like an approaching express train. After several hours of bombardment one night, my sister-in-law made tea and brought the tray into the lounge. As she was about to put it down we heard the sound of an approaching express train. At once all the males present dived under the table. We crawled out shamefaced, after the bomb exploded; safely for us, but not for the six houses in Station Avenue which it destroyed. Afterwards my sister-in-law found it highly amusing that she had simply stood there, incapable of jettisoning the tea tray. She wouldn't have wanted to waste a precious tea ration.

Tea was vital to the British War effort. One of the sounds my mother feared most was a knock on the door telling us that our inebriated neighbour "Inky" had arrived to make sure that Dr. and Mrs. Datta, whom he loved dearly, were alright. For him, mother served the strongest tea ever made, before gently ushering him on his way to his many night caps. He usually embarrassed my father by constantly reminding him that when he had served in India, (presumably in the Police) he had actually met Gandhi.

'People all called him Mahatma' he slurred. 'but that was wrong. His real name was 'Mohandas'. Mohandas K. Gandhi he was called. He was a lovely man. And so are you too, my dear Dr. Datta, and Mrs Datta, and David and Albion. I love you all. And never worry about the bombs. Old Gerry will look after you.'

The next day, his gesture of defiance was to fly a skull and cross bones from his flagpole. This was an improvement on the Swastika he had once run up, but been asked to take down by the Air Raid Warden.

On one occasion I and my brother climbed the fire-escape to the top of Snowdon House from where we had a grandstand view of the Blitz. That night the centre of town was particularly badly hit. Fires were raging all over my mother's favourite shopping area. Even from a distance the inferno was such that one could see flaming sparks rising into the clouds. Later I realised that this was what was left of Bristol's mediaeval heritage. Nothing burns so merrily as ancient richly carved Tudor timberwork. Not even walls are left standing. Sometimes a searchlight would touch on a bomber; and at once every one in the area swung in that direction, and every gun altered its fire accordingly. One plane certainly did go down near Portishead.

At the height of the action I glanced at my brother. Instead of excitement, there were tears in his eyes. An emotional man, 12 years my senior, he loved his city. He understood the true horror of it all, and he knew that for him especially, this was just the beginning.

At one point an incendiary hit the gas holder a mile or so away. There was no explosion but a single flare of gaslight that lit up the area as though the sun had burst through. It was bright enough to read a book by. And when after several hours the moon did come out and the clouds dispersed, the night sky was a chicken pox rash of shell bursts so dense that it seemed no aircraft could possibly have got through it.

On the following Monday, one went to school and saw the result. There was little left of the shopping area. Department stores, theatres, the skating rink, cinemas, had vanished. Many roads were simply blocked by rubble that took weeks to clear. The museum near my school had gone, and with it stuffed lions and the remains of a priceless ichthyosaurus were deposited back into the river. The exquisite 'Dutch House' which had hardly been damaged was pulled down by a pioneer platoon whose officer did not understand the corbelled nature of Sixteenth century building, and thought it was leaning over dangerously because of a bomb blast.

We learned to live with bomb sites for many years to come, and botany teachers pointed out how readily rose bay willow herb colonised such places. At school the collection of souvenir shell splinters became a competition. An unexploded incendiary bomb was a piece de resistance. The raids continued at irregular intervals throughout the winter and well into 1941. 'Bomb stories' became standard entertainment and in my class was a boy with memorable entertaining skills who could take off Churchill's famous wartime speeches to perfection. "We shall fight them on the beaches" was rasped out while waiting for the French teacher, and 'sotto voce,' during physics classes.

There were several daylight raids at which we were mostly accommodated in the school shelter. The school 'Sergeant', ex R.S.M. Middlecote, stood guard at the entrance and one boy vowed he collected a piece of shrapnel which had bounced off the Sergeant's chest. Others were accommodated in the basement of the Biology section of the University which contained numbers of animal embryos preserved in glass jars. The smell was not too good and the ambiance less than desirable in the context of death and destruction. Some senior boys were also allowed to volunteer for fire-watching duties, but I lived too far out for this truly adult activity. I volunteered to become an ARP Messenger, but my services were never called on.

The ultimate measure of prestige was the kind of steel helmet a boy might be able to acquire. Initially it was possible to buy imitation helmets of a fairly inadequate pattern, and it was better not to be seen with one of these. My own machinations in this area finally bore fruit when I found that my father had two 'proper' steel helmets, one of them painted Civil Defence White. Soon it became mine. One carried it about, strung over a military type gas mask with Goggle eyes. I felt I could hold the entire Wehrmacht at bay.

The Wagnerian dramas of the night raids were interspersed with daylight attacks of which we saw little since we were in the school. These tended to be more concentrated on specific targets like Avonmouth Docks or the Filton aircraft works, and they brought their own kind of horror. My friend Ray Smith reported seeing a Heinkel machine gunning the length of the Gloucester Road. It then dropped its bomb on Filton which exploded at the entrance of the air raid shelter killing many people.

My own experience led to a rapid maturing of feelings about war. I arrived home from school one day around 4.30 p.m. and saw a large concourse of fire engines, ambulances and Civil Defence workers at the entrance to the hospital. I hurried home, to be met at the door by my mother who said;

'It's alright, your father's alright. A plane's come down on the hospital but there's nothing to worry about.'

'German or British?' I asked anxiously. She said she thought German. I telephoned my father and got permission to go and visit the scene.

My father's office opened on to a small courtyard with just one tree in it. There was a deep hole in the tarmac, and all about were

The Messerschmitt that crashed on Stapleton Hospital
(Photo courtesy of Bristol United Press)

scattered blackened pieces of aircraft wreckage, none of it large enough to be recognisable, except for the cannons and machine guns which lay to one side. There were disordered piles of ammunition, mostly spent, which included 9mm and 20mm canon shells. Air raid wardens and members of staff were attempting to sort out the mess. There were hoses from the fire tenders and water swirled everywhere. Above all came the complicated smell of gun smoke, fuel oil and presumably burnt human flesh. My father was in his office writing a report. I was recognised and no-one questioned my presence, but one of the workers pointed to a wheelbarrow, covered with a tarpaulin.

'I shouldn't look under that,' he said grimly.

When I had the scene in focus, adolescent instincts surfaced and I thought greedily of souvenirs. I couldn't quite see myself turning up at school with a whole German machine gun, but there was plenty more besides to whet the appetite. I pocketed a few cartridge cases. Nobody told me off.

My father came out of his office and greeted me. 'It missed you by inches, dad,' I said.

'There was a man actually in the courtyard', he said. 'He saw it coming down and flattened himself against the tree. Didn't even get a scratch'.

He went on to explain that he had been working in his office when this huge explosion happened.

'Goodness, we've been hit by a bomb!' I thought. I rushed to open the door and then heard bullets going off. 'My God, they're shooting at us,' I thought, and slammed the door shut.

When the 'shooting' stopped he inched the door open and went gingerly forth, realising that the sounds had been bullets exploding in the heat.

I spent an hour or so at the scene, then, before leaving, yielded to the urge to look into the barrow. It was merely a congealed mass that had once been a human being. I replaced the tarpaulin quickly. Then, as I was about to go home, something nearby under a mound of debris caught my eye. It was a piece of cloth with some yellow braid on it. A piece of uniform! I grabbed it, rolled it up and left the hospital. No-one at school would ever have a souvenir like this!

At home I guiltily hid it in an outhouse. Next day, I thought confession might be good for the soul. I told my mother and handed it to her. She was utterly horrified.

'David,' she said, shaking her head, 'he was some mother's son.' 'Perhaps,' I thought, 'but he nearly killed my father,' But I said nothing. My mother fetched a bucket of water and put the material in it. The water turned brown. It was proof enough of my ineptitude. I never took the uniform to school. Soon afterwards it disappeared, and I never discussed the matter again.

My father ended the gruesome story by expressing the view that there had been two men in the plane's crew because he had picked different pieces of scalp off his wall, some with blond hair, and some with dark hair.

The next day a Hurricane Pilot, Flying Officer Royce, from Bristol 501 squadron arrived to claim the tailplane of the Messerschmitt 110 he had shot down.

For me it was an end to any lingering notion of the romance of war, particularly when I learned that the German pilot had been buried with full military honours at Greenbank Cemetry in a grave quite close that of my mother's mother.

The Bristol Blitz lasted for nearly 2 years with diminishing effectiveness. The real damage had all been done in the first few months. And by a sad irony the last raid of all was as unhappy as any. In August 1942 in daylight, a lone Heinkel dropped a 500lb bomb on the city centre, destroying five double decker buses and killing forty four people.

By then "Bomber" Harris, was seeking Churchill's permission to repay the Germans in kind. We and the Americans did it with "round the clock", thousand bomber raids on every major German city, not excluding Dresden.

After the Blitz. My mother's favourite shopping street.
(*Photo courtesy of Reece Winstone*)

Chapter 11

By the spring of 1942, British morale had reached its lowest point so far. The RAF had beaten off the Luftwaffe, but all major British cities had been severely damaged. We had sunk the Graf Spee and the Bismarck, but the pride of the Navy, the Hood, had been blown to bits and at least seven other warships had gone down including the Prince of Wales and the Ark Royal. On dry land Dunkirk had been followed by retreat in North Africa and total surrender in Singapore. Brave men with no uniforms kept us fed via North Atlantic convoys; the Merchant Navy suffered enormous losses and their sacrifices have only recently been acknowledged by the be-ribboned functionaries that surround Buckingham Palace.

For me one incident caused near despair. Two great enemy battleships were moored in Brest under concrete and had survived all British air attacks. Then the Germans decided to remove them to the safety of Jutland. They came out at the head of a flotilla and sailed clear up the English Channel within sight of the white cliffs of Dover. It was an escape so daring that it took us totally by surprise. All we could do was send up nine ancient Swordfish biplanes with torpedoes after them. Six were shot down. When the news broke we were appalled. Where were our Beaufighters, our destroyers, our motor torpedo boats? It seemed as though the Germans had knocked on our windows and thumbed their noses at us. It was an insult to the memory of Nelson.

Soon after that the call came to my brother put on an Army Officer's uniform and amid sombre farewells, he left for an unknown destination.

As the year progressed the American declaration of war which followed Pearl Harbour, began to bear fruit. More and more 'Yanks' were seen around town, fit, well dressed and with an unquestionable appeal to local girls. 'Oversexed, overpaid and over here' was an embittered response from local males. They had money and plenty of transport with their jeeps and their huge camouflaged 'Rio' trucks. Peter Nichols, the future playwright, claimed he practised future 'drag acts' with his chums, parading past one nearby camp in high heeled shoes, with handbags. There was however no question about their intention to stay and see the job through. They built air bases all over Britain, and at Frenchay a much needed casualty hospital that functions well today. Unfortunately they also brought with them home grown prejudices and in Bristol a race riot took place between black and white which lasted two days, and led to the intervention of carbine carrying G.I 'Snowballs'. The local police, armed with whistles and bicycles, simply left them to it and cordoned off traffic to the town centre. Bristolians were learning something about the world their own ancestors had helped to create.

The other far more crucial happening was on the mysterious Eastern front, where the tough sounding Marshall Zhukov declared that enough was enough and the Germans would never be allowed to take Stalingrad or Leningrad, no matter what the cost in Russian lives. He kept his word in all respects. In the Kursk salient, tens of thousands died. In Stalingrad, the Russians fought house by house, until at last they began to advance.

By October, Bomber Harris had persuaded Churchill that Germany could be defeated by aerial bombardment and B17's and Lancasters had begun the cold blooded destruction of German cities. At the same time an extraordinary General called Bernard Montgomery brought off a surprising British victory at El Alamein which thrilled the allies and led to Churchill's famous comment that "this is not the end; nor even the beginning of the end; but it is the end of the beginning."

Before very long we learned that my brother too was in North Africa, having landed with his Division in Tunisia. We had no idea what he might be going through; his wife wrote regularly but replies were slow in coming and heavily censored. In fact he saw action of the bloodiest kind at something that became known as "The Battle of Longstop Hill." British tanks led the way up a mountain in 'line ahead formation' and were picked off by German 88 mm guns. As he himself advanced he found the bodies of several Germans killed by bayonet wounds. He himself was tempted to remove a pair of Zeiss binoculars from one of them, but became suspicious and resisted. A few moments later he heard the explosion as a booby trap was detonated.

He had in fact arrived in time for Rommel's 'last stand' in Africa. As the Eighth Army advanced from the East, the German hero was recalled, became involved in the plot to assassinate Hitler, and committed suicide.

My father's attitude to the war was one of total commitment. I myself took a certain pride on hearing of any Indian Army achievements, like the several V.C's that were awarded to men of the Fourth Indian Division in Africa. We closed our minds to the fact that a renegade Indian army had been formed to assist the Japanese in Malaya. It was also too soon for us to know about the greatest Indian heroine Noor Khan who (after overcoming normal British racial prejudice) had joined the S.A.S., was parachuted into France and spent many dangerous months organising the Resistance and sending back radio messages. Finally caught, she was shot in Dachau. She was awarded a posthumous George Cross.

My father had pinned up a large Daily Telegraph war map on the wall of his study. On it he had indicated with pins the disposition of the German and Russian forces confronting each other over a front many hundreds of miles long.

One day I made so bold as to remonstrate with him 'Dad, why have you put up a map of the Russian front, why not North African where Albion is fighting?'

His explanation was as always patient and detailed.

'There are over a thousand divisions locked in battle in Russia,' he said. 'This is where the war will be won or lost. The whole future of Europe, and maybe the world, will be decided here.'

It seemed even Churchill did not disagree with him. He caused a special sword to be made, the sword of Stalingrad, and awarded it to his one time enemy, Stalin.

Eventually we had news from my brother. His unit had joined the combined British and American force that had been brought to

Captain Albion Datta, on his way to meet Rommel

Tunisia with the intention of striking East, capturing Tripoli, and cutting off Rommel's retreat from Libya.

It was a classic piece of strategic paper planning that almost went disastrously wrong. The first American attack had failed, the allies were beaten back at the Kasserine Pass with over 6,000 men lost. Only after 6 months of bitter fighting and a build up of troops to outnumber the enemy by at least ten to one was the objective achieved. Even years later my brother gave only reluctant glimpses of what he had experienced. The history writers and movie makers pass rapidly over this operation.

The left wing press in Britain kept up their campaign to open a second front in France, but the allies wisely took the more circuitous route via Italy. While my brother's unit was waiting to invade, the officers lived in a spacious Tunisian villa. One of their number was a Captain Morse Brown who had been an artist with the Illustrated London News. He drew a fine portrait of my brother and decorated the walls with murals depicting his colleagues in Roman armour, embarking like Hannibal on his great invasion of Italy. Among the British, culture and humour could never be supressed for long.

A long silence followed until we received a letter containing a neatly coded message. "We have landed in Italy" it said, "And I hope to have a nice egg for my breakfast." It was my father who finally solved it. There was a well-known breed of hen called a 'Leghorn'.

'Leghorn', my father said, 'is the English version of the Italian Livorno. He is at Livorno.'

He was on his way home. However the route lay via Monte Cassino and instead of Italian ice-cream there would be morphine injections and amputations, a desperate last stand by the Germans, and as always, death by 'friendly fire'. More than once my brother had to dig a trench to avoid being killed by the U.S. Air Force.

My father's service on the 'Home Front' continued to consist of First Aid classes two or three times weekly, driving through unlit streets with masked headlights. Often he would manage to drop my mother off at one of her evening classes where her embroidery reached new heights. My sister in law taught cookery, and this became a form of 'mime'; since there were few ingredients to spare, pastry and cake making were often performed either with plaster or nothing at all. Nevertheless it is received wisdom that we were a well nourished generation with lots of sound advice from experts on clever ways to serve cabbage, carrots and leeks. The shortage of sugar was good for our teeth, and free school milk attained a level of a religious ritual. Fish always seemed plentiful thanks to the courage of British trawlermen. Our bodies and bones generally were probably far better then than those of our parents. Carrots, we were told, would help us see at night and become good night fighter pilots.

Nor was there any diminution of political activity. My father continued to give talks to youth clubs and schools, gently easing in a message for Indian Independence. The party associations and Unions tended to be in the hands of the old campaigners, and there was a distinct sense that when "this lot is over" there would be some changes made. All political agendas stressed the need for a proper state provided Health Service, better schools, more access to Universities: And everyone who voted Labour knew that by the end of the war people with new ideas would have to take the place of the Churchills, the Edens and Beaverbrooks.

I remember asking my father what he felt about Patriotism.

'When a country is down, it is a virtue' he replied. 'But when a country is on top it becomes a vice.' England certainly needed every ounce of it; and, for different reasons, he felt the same about India. One thing my father also learned was that Indian Independence and Colonial freedom could not be taken for granted among Labour supporters. There were still plenty of workers who were brought up to believe in the Empire; if the Indians were to spin their own cotton, wouldn't this put British workers out of jobs ? There was also racial prejudice. When, after the war, the first West Indians arrived to work on the Bristol buses, the staff threatened a walkout. An unsung hero called Stephenson replied by organising a boycott of the buses. The T.G.W.U. called off the strike.

My mother wrote regularly to her two sisters, Mabel in California and Doris in Jamaica, a nurse who had married a Jamaican and settled in Kingston with no intention of ever returning to England. They wished us good fortune and gave us plenty of invitations to visit when the war ended. But we had little in common; the idea of staying in a California where I would not be allowed to go to the cinema did not appeal. And I knew that if I should one day travel, it was the call of the East that would have priority over that of the West. To this day I have met only one Indian cousin, and no Jamaican ones.

One unexpected result of the war was an introduction to physical labour. Manpower was in very short supply, and older boys were invited to take part in "Harvest Camps". We were paid anything up to sixpence a day, and knew we were helping the "War effort". We slept under canvas and took on some of the worst jobs in farming, lifting potatoes with fork and bucket, hacking down thistles with sickles, and generally breaking our backs. We mucked out cowsheds in pouring rain, and at some camps, fancied ourselves as lumberjacks, cutting pit props in a heatwave and trying to clear off the sweat and tar in a nearby mill pond. Our most elegant billet was at the vast Horlicks mansion in the Cotswolds where the owners obligingly turned out their string of racehorses allowing us to bed down two in a stall, with palliasses and plenty of fresh straw. We were allowed to swim in the mansion's swimming pool while American Officers watched us, Martinis in hand, no doubt saying good things to the hostess about our British determination to win the War.

It remains a matter of pride that in later years I could look some grizzled old son of the soil in the eye, and tell him that I too knew how to stook a cornfield.

Less romantic was the call to come in and scrub the school floors during the holidays, the cleaners being mostly in factories or the army. One wonders how such an idea would be greeted by today's Staff and unions.

One sacred British institution, much praised by Henry James, was that of afternoon tea. There was a steady stream of visitors to Snowdon House, often strongly political but sometimes merely people paying their respects. They ranged from University lecturers to Sikh pedlars with suitcases containing cheap jewellery. No Indian was ever turned away, whatever his status. More sophisticated were members of the British Soviet Friendship society, in those days a flourishing body, and there was even a memorable visit from a friend of Paul Robeson who was then on a politically motivated tour of Britain.

Afternoon tea allowed my mother to offer token nourishment in the form of Ritz-style cucumber or tomato sandwiches, without the stress of rationing- hit dinner invitations. Visitors went on their way feeling welcomed, but not bloated.

The household was unquestionably dominated by my father's political commitments. Such was his sparkling persona and conversational fluidity that my mother accepted her role as a devoted acolyte. The term she tended to use was "general dogsbody." To escape from unremitting political talk she cultivated her own little circle of ladies, but in the end these tailed off. More than once a friend became a sad widow when a husband was posted "missing in action"

There was however, one little occasion of near insurrection which led to a wonderful vignette of English social history. Her favourite cousin Wilf (of Pontypridd library fame) had a son Vivian who had been a regular in the R.A.F. His service career was now ended, much of it having been spent on the North West frontier of India, He had retired to live in a Cotswold village well known to Laurie Lee, called Sheepscombe. Here he had met the daughter of a retired Indian Army colonel who lived in a nearby village called Cranham, where there was about to be a wedding to which we were cordially invited. Nothing would have prevented my mother from going to it, but my father was unfortunately unable to attend. I do not recall what commitment made it impossible for him to go, but if it was a diplomatic excuse I could certainly hazard an explanation. He would have been more than somewhat aware of the part played by the British military establishment in holding back his country's progress towards independence. He would probably have felt as welcome at such an event as a brown version of Banquo at the banquet. So my mother decided she would have to go alone. She had long ago given up driving, even if there were enough petrol coupons for the trip, so she set about finding some means of public transport. Her great, great grandfather had regularly made such a journey by gig to buy his rum in Bristol, so it ought to be possible, and the girl who had run away to London from Seventh Day Adventist parents was not to be thwarted. To her delight she ascertained that she could get a train from Temple Meads to Stroud; and thereafter, wonder of wonders, there was actually a branch line to Cranham itself.

The journey proved to be one that belongs to a bygone age of railway romance; to the misty era of McNight Kauffer posters, bracing Skegness or classy Eastbourne. On her arrival at Stroud station she sought out the Station Master. He, the dignified fount of all local railway knowledge, flourished his watch chain and said;

'Yes Madam, we do have a train to Cranham. It is waiting now at platform two, and leaves in twenty two minutes.' My mother crossed the bridge to be confronted by a little tank engine, steaming keenly. As she approached it, the driver descended and introduced himself. My mother explained her mission.

'Oh yes lady,' he said,'this is the train you want. I know about Mr. Cowdray's wedding. We'll be there in time for the ceremony. Then the reception should be over by about four. If that suits you, we'll wait for you and bring you back.'

At this point he became technical and explained that it was a single track, so the train would come backwards as a "pusher".

'We call this train the Dudbridge Donkey. Hope you have a nice time.'

My mother had a wonderful time.

When the great accountant Beeching slaughtered the British rail network after the war, he hung, drew and quartered it body and soul. Edward Thomas preserved its spirit in a famously evocative poem, "Adlestrop." John Betjeman wept tears over the old Somerset and Dorset, at Evercreech junction. And Flanders and Swan sang the last lament;

"No more we'll go from Blandford Forum to Mortee..hoe
On the slow, slow train...."

They were happy highways where we went, and cannot come again.

Chapter 12

The concept of the unattainable loved one is a well established literary cliche. At the age of fourteen mine was a tall slim girl with long fair plaits, who wore a blue mackintosh and lived in Manor Road. I would see her waiting at the bus stop, or walking home. The merest glimpse caused the well documented intake of breath, increased heart beat and so on. I was guilty of taking unnecessary bicycle trips in the hope of seeing her. I never spoke, she never acknowledged me, and I felt a permanent sense of loss. She would be astonished to know how I felt. The image remains.

There were other attractive girls not far away, but they were older and even less interested in me. Senior male friends however made much headway with one of them. Her name was Maureen and she lived in a house that backed onto a nearby lane. On long summer evenings they became entangled in passionate embraces until her mother's voice was heard at high decibel levels in a strange Lancashire accent, reminiscent of Gracie Fields, calling "Cum in our Maureen! Our Maureen, cum in this minute!" Obviously she knew when the point of no return was getting close, and it also taught me that there were other people in the British Isles who had modes of address very different from our soft West Country mumblings.

Fortunately school made such demands on one, with Latin declensions, quadratic equations, French vocabulary, grammar and syntax, that there was little time for romantic moping. I was doing well but not brilliantly, with decided weaknesses in maths and science, and I had to struggle to keep up the standards imposed by a truly excellent group of teachers. Similarly in sport; I could run quite fast but there were others who beat me. I enjoyed Rugby and regularly joined my friend Austin Davis in the school team or in opposing house teams.

The advantage of being at a day school was clear. There was nearby a well organised youth club where one could learn authentic Victor Sylvester dance steps. More appealing though were records of up to the minute American swing bands that gave us our generation's music from Glen Miller, Basie, Goodman and the almost worn flat favourite, Woody Herman's "Wood-chopper's Ball."

Occasionally trips were organised to a decrepit farm in the wilds near Iron Acton, whose owner kept a string of ill kempt riding hacks on which we jogged perilously along Cotswold by-ways.

At last I succeeded in establishing a regular liaison with a girl called Brenda. We took long cycle rides together into the country, and I practised my first faltering efforts at making an impression. Having acquired a smattering of appreciation of classical music, I called Cesar Franck to my aid, and asked her if she did not think his Symphony in D Minor a wonderful piece of music? If I had intended to score a point, I was quickly defeated. She agreed that it was, and then asked if I knew the 'Symphonic Variations.' I had to admit I didn't. At once she went over to the attack.

'Oh dear,' she said, 'I'm surprised you don't know the Symphonic Variations. They're the best thing he ever wrote. An absolutely wonderful composition.'

My moonlit cycle rides with Brenda ended soon afterwards. Not wholly because of Cesar Franck. But I developed a highly guarded attitude to girls who knew more that I did about a subject. It remains; and there are so many of them.

I never knew what happened to Brenda; but if someone tells me she became Headmistress of a leading Girl's School I shall be highly satisfied and not in the least surprised.

Sex and Romance were of course two utterly distinct concepts, they had been so since the 'Roman de la Rose', continued through Victorian times and remained so until, as Larkin put it so memorably, "the Beatles first L.P." They were matters of equal concern, but utterly different in kind, and falling in love must never be sullied by lustful urges. Sheer ignorance was of course a dominant factor, but one re-calls the compulsion to explain the differences between male and female being present at the earliest age. Brief question and answer discussions took place among boys when only six or seven years old; totally fallacious theories were put forward and one did one's best not to ask again. But the subject was only repressed, and since there was no structured education on the subject, finding the facts was largely accidental.

In my case, I blundered about like an old man who has lost his glasses. The presence of 'Grey's Anatomy' in my father's library only seemed to deepen the mystery. Then one day various cousins came to stay and I found myself briefly in league with a female of my own age. In a garden shed I satisfied her inquisitiveness and she offered to make a reciprocal demonstration. To do so she offered to stand on an orange box, since visibility was otherwise too restricted to make it a fair exchange. I was hugely grateful for her initiative and the fact that she went on to become the wife of a world famous religious leader in California has ensured that I have kept the matter sub judice until this moment.

Even so, I continued to be a puzzled adolescent on the mechanics of the thing until my brother's wife took pity on me and laughingly explained how it was done. I remained grateful to her for years to come.

If music is said to be the food of love I found some support for the notion. My friend Austin was making sound progress as a pianist, and on one occasion arranged for two highly gifted acquaintances, a pianist and a violinist to give a memorable performance of Mendelsohn's Violin Concerto in a neighbour's tiny front room. Sadly, my own efforts lagged far behind his. Encouraged by my mother I continued to take lessons from my brother's wife's youngest sister, Mollie, a qualified piano teacher. I was utterly bored by having to learn the language of crochets and quavers, and when I came to learn the inevitable 'first steps' my deficiencies became painfully apparent. It was always an effort to translate the dots on a page of music to the appropriate black and white ivories on the keyboard; and when it came to making the left hand play something entirely different from what the right hand was playing, and yet make them somehow synchronise with each other, I struggled horribly. Neurologists must by now have discovered a complex of cells akin to the hypocanthus which musicians possess, and which I surely lacked. 'Walking and chewing gum' I could manage, but not a great deal beyond that where music was concerned.

However the burden of this confessional relates to the qualities of my teacher rather than my inadequacies. Molly, at age 24 or so, was petite, curvaceous, and red haired, with sparkling eyes and a ready smile. She exuded a warmth that could bring a glow to a winter's day. Her little flat was near my school in Redland, and I called in once a week, to be greeted by a welcome that I could only take to indicate profound fondness. On one particular afternoon I followed her into the lounge and hung my satchel on a chair near the piano. Then just for a moment I stood and looked at her. For those few seconds she too stood and smiled at me. It flashed through my racing brain that I was within an arm's length of making a move that could end my fifteen years of raging puzzlement about the true nature of all the differences between men and women.

Then I thought about Len. I took my place at the piano and tried to concentrate. Len, her husband, was a tall, soft spoken solicitor, respected and greatly liked by all the family. He was in the 14th Army in Burma, and probably at that moment wading through some waist-high jungle swamp, trying to kill a Japanese who was trying to kill him. We prayed he would come home safe, and I was much relieved that when he did I would be able to look him in the eye and shake his hand.

In the event, I remained true to the frustrations of the Larkin principle for years to come. Towards the end of my school career I formed an emotional attachment to an attractive local girl called June who lived locally. By then I was a car driver, and even a motor-bike owner. Many trips were taken to West Country hostelries, we played lots of English style tennis, and became regarded as an item. Only one brief moment revealed a shadow over the relationship. One day she admitted with much embarrassment that her father, who had seen service in India, was not entirely favourably disposed to our relationship. It was one of a thankfully small number of instances I was to experience of racial prejudice directed against me. She made clear that she had no intention of being influenced by it, and I was egotistical enough not to let it bother me. Arrogance can be a useful defence. Our relationship continued until I was called up, joined the R.A.F., and was posted to the Far East. By the time of my return she had been, as she put it, "swept off her feet" by a returning Fleet Air Arm Fighter Pilot who had won a medal for gallantry. They were rapidly engaged, and then married. My friends and I had been born just a little too late to become war heroes, even if we had been made of the right stuff, which was by no means certain. Her dad must have been hugely relieved.

Failure to become any kind of pianist in no way diminished my love of music, particularly the popular variety which embraced swing, boogie woogie, and the great show classics like "Somewhere over the Rainbow" which had just arrived from the States and which I hummed happily while riding my new bicycle, and which still tugs the heart strings. However here I have to confess to taking what some would call a path of utter perversion in that area, and which caused my father total dismay.

The most popular stage and film performer of the day was a Northern gent called George Formby, and I fell for him, hook, line and plectrum. As a comic he was certainly no wit; merely a clown with no red nose, but a row of gravestones for teeth. He developed a line of somewhat risque songs about window cleaners and Chinese laundrymen which are in the time honoured English tradition of Marie Lloyd songs and Donald McGill postcards. But it was George's playing of what he called his "Banjulele" that really turned me on. The banjo is an instrument with a hallowed history in the USA; it allows a tremendous percussive beat, together with complex and melodic fingering. It is far too awkward for a comedian to clown with, so George had developed a kind of "Banjolele" which allowed wonderful strumming and quick chord changes. It fitted his songs perfectly, and aficionados flocked to see his films. My two great passions merged when he made a film about the RAF called "It's in the Air". I saw it more times than I care to admit and once even persuaded my father to take the family. The film confirmed his worst fears. He was too kind a parent to voice them, but his private worries about me must have mounted sky high. Had he fathered a moron for a son ? Was it really worth while spending good money on my education ? He must have prayed that I would grow out of it; but he also knew that he might one day have to go and see my Headmaster and ask if somehow they were failing me.

My only conceivable defence for this cultural aberration (in my adolescence, let it be said) is to point to the hundreds of Gorge Formby clubs which thrive, fifty years on, across Northern England, with thousands of adult males strumming their "banjoleles", singing about window cleaners, and greeting each other with the immortal words;

"Eeh ! Turned out nice again !"

Chapter 13

In 1943 a new headmaster called John Garrett was appointed to Bristol Grammar School.

I first saw him standing at the foot of the stone staircase waiting for Mr. Cheyney the organist to finish the prelude which would announce his ascent to preside over morning prayers in the Great Hall. A fair haired, well built man in a long scholar's gown, he was appropriately magisterial; a figure to impress older boys and intimidate younger ones.

I was allowed to miss morning prayers, along with Young (Catholic) and Alexander (Jewish). It was assumed that my father practised some exotic oriental rites, and I was happy to foster the illusion because it gave me an extra fifteen minutes to get to school from 6 miles away. In fact my father's family had not been practising Hindus since the time of the Indian Mutiny.

John Garrett would prove to have an immense armoury of talents, as an administrator, an imaginative innovator, a talented teacher, and ultimately a firm friend. He came to Bristol with an impressive record. In 1935 he had been appointed the first headmaster of a newly built London school, Raynes Park County school designed to be a showpiece of progressive State educational planning, and he was presented with the task of making it a success. In the event he turned dream into reality, with a high achievement level in Matriculation and Higher Schools Certificate. He developed clubs and societies and fostered the highest possible standards of school drama. Wide and gifted contacts gave him much assistance in all such matters; not many schools can boast a school song and motto composed by W.H. Auden, but Raynes Park did. As a school it began at once to produce future performers in the arts and the media far in excess of the numbers normally expected from a South London suburb.

At Bristol his first and most revolutionary move was to introduce school lunches. Today when no school would be allowed to exist without its dinners and dinner ladies, it may seem hard to imagine that this was an epoch making move. Except in the very poorest areas, school in the thirties was for feeding brains, not bodies; devotion to arithmetic and English grammar excluded all other considerations. But to Garrett, brought up on the joyful stimulus of "Dinner in Hall" at an Oxford College it seemed a besetting fault that a good school should be without such a productive and cohesive environment. The Bristol Grammar School Hall, though merely Victorian, offered a wonderful setting.

So he spent a mind-bending Summer with governors, accountants, constructors, caterers, and suppliers of equipment. And then one day we came to school, and behold, there was no more call for sardine sandwiches. Several hundred of us could sit and eat and chat together. Previous headmasters might have wished it so: John Garrett made it so. At table he was available to all. He would sit with any group of any age, modernists, classicists, or scientists, and initiate table talk of a kind few of them experienced at home. He wanted to bring the banter and brilliance he had known in his Oxford years to the normally tongue tied sons of lower middle class middle England.

'David,' he said to me once, 'at least you come from a home where people talk'.

Anything was permissible in the name of Wit, and on one occasion he jabbed his spoon at a plate of Semolina which had a dab of jam in the middle and chortled,

'Look. It's just like a breast. And there's the nipple in the middle.' The sons of office managers were to have their horizons widened in as many ways as possible. Probably his most all pervading characteristic was sheer unbounded enthusiasm for everything he became involved in. This alone would have made him a quite exemplary teacher, and although his own degree was in History, he concentrated on English literature and Shakespeare in particular. It could hardly be otherwise since at Oxford he had formed close bonds with W.H. Auden, Neville Coghill, Spender, C.S. Lewis, MacNeice and others who went on to form a literary Pantheon of their day. After leaving Oxford he and Auden had published "The Poet's Tongue". It was a self confessed way to make some money, but it was a superb work and quite supplanted Palgrave's Golden Treasury. Inevitably he seized the opportunity to take the Sixth Form Classes in English. This might have led to a staffing resentment, since there had been for many years a wonderful Senior English master called "Fred" Perry. But "Uncle Fred" was a paragon of urbanity and an amicable arrangement was quickly reached. It was he who actually introduced us to the joy of Geoffrey Chaucer, and led us through "Macbeth". He showed us how the daunting appearance of blank verse need hold no fears, he sorted out all the textual mysteries, conveyed all the power of Elizabethan drama, and dozens of boys who would otherwise have rated the Swan of Avon an excruciating old bore, learned to place him at the pinnacle of their value ratings.

For the Sixth form, Garrett was left with either Hamlet or Browning, and for him there was no choice. 'You can't get boys interested in Browning' he said. But Fred Perry managed it, and I can still pick up a Browning poem and enjoy its devious storytelling and quirky originality. "Hamlet" taught by Garrett on the other hand, was like a religious experience. For the first time we learned that problems were not just a matter of unfriendly people dropping bombs on us; they could rise from within ourselves and bring any one of us to a state of paralysis, and might even remove the will to live. Week after week he set us essays on the play, and the discussions that followed could raise the most inhibited of adolescent minds, to unexpected levels of psychological analysis. He marked our essays with deep commitment and in my case, favourably enough to make me feel I had written something that he enjoyed and respected.

Nothing in the rest of my erratic educational career would ever give me such satisfaction as the essays I wrote for Garrett on "Hamlet".

His lectures relied heavily on the revered "Prefaces to Shakespeare" by the Edwardian actor, critic and dramatist, Harley Granville Barker. We knew little of that, and had I been more sophisticated, I might have interjected "Sir, my father actually saw Granville Barker on stage in 1910." Had I done so, Garrett would have purred with delight at the idea of one of his boys being so close to greatness (in fact his brief experience of the London stage, was a favourite memory of my father's. He had tried, but failed, to get into RADA, and years later, on a visit to Bristol, when I tried to persuade him to come and see Laurence Olivier's "Hamlet", he snorted derisively, 'Olivier? Olivier? I have seen Beerbohm Tree's Hamlet!')

Although all our work was governed by exam syllabuses, the best teachers always found ways to introduce subjects that would widen our vision and deepen our appreciation. In the case of John Garrett I recall whole classes extolling the quality of the poetry of Thomas Hardy, Rupert Brook, D.H. Lawrence, his friend John Betjeman, and even W.S. Gilbert. His next move was dramatic, in every sense of the term. He succeeded in luring to Bristol a man he had known at Raynes Park, a man of extraordinary gifts and immense charm called Frank Beecroft. Beecroft had been the motive force in raising school drama to new heights, and he was now ready to do the same for Bristol Grammar School. First however we knew him as my Form master, and a teacher of French poetry. A sufficient challenge, one might think, but here a whole new dimension was revealed. Most of Beecroft's classes began with a period of badinage between himself and the three leading school wits, who sat in the front row. On the Radio at that time there were plenty of great comedy shows like ITMA, but what took place in 6M compared with anything the professionals could provide, and was quite as surreal. Wisecracks and ripostes shot to and fro like a demented game of Battledore, while the whole class rocked and applauded. Beecroft held court like a Victorian Master of Ceremonies, until, the period time almost over, and grinning with sheer pleasure, he would pick up a text book and say.

'Well we really must do some work, we really must.'

It remains a mystery how any of us could get to grips with de Vigny and Lamartine, but a surprising number did, and the exam results were more than satisfactory.

In addition to charisma and charm, Beecroft brought with him rare musical gifts as a pianist, violinist, and amateur conductor. We had the use of the University music theatre and he arranged performances by people like Natasha Litvin, and Max Rostal himself. Garrett described him as "certainly of Wigmore Hall standard." Only once did he tread on my pro-Soviet toes by giving vent to an outburst against Shostakovitch, "that complete and utter charlatan". There was also a small nucleus of jazz fanatics who would insist on irritatingly tapping their feet when he played Mozart. He tolerated them with a benign smile. After all he had been to the first night of Walton's "Facade."

Beecroft's first production, naturally enough was "Hamlet". Even the most confident of producers could not make the play a success without an actor of sensitivity and conviction; and here he was remarkable lucky. In Sixth Classical was a tall, good looking boy of thoughtful demeanour. His name was Charles Boyes and he came from a strongly religious background. Equally important he had the capacity (notoriously lacking in many TV actors) to learn lines of more than five seconds duration. The mix was complete, and the result was memorable. Neville Coghill came to see it, and it was praised in some national media. For me it became the criterion by which to judge any Hamlet. So would he go on to become a rival to Olivier ? If a glittering West End career was on offer, it was not for him. Charles entered a Catholic seminary and few of us outside of that world, heard of him thereafter.

Beecroft had to work hard to maintain his first success. He discovered John Beadle who made an excellent Falstaff, and John Garrett's social standing reached new heights when Queen Mary, who had been evacuated to Badminton during the war, came to one production and sat with him. He delighted to relate how she kept elbowing him in the ribs to emphasize a point she had made when the play began. It would have been a matter of much sorrow for him however to realise that the one boy from school who went on to make a truly great success in the theatre world, left at about this time and took no part in school productions; indeed the headmaster was probably scarcely aware of his existence. He was Peter Nichols.

Beecroft's talents helped to establish Bristol as a good place to learn about theatre. The Old Vic Theatre School was just making a world wide name for itself, and beginning to produce people like Peter O'Toole, Brian Blessed, Daniel Day Lewis, Jeremy Irons, Patricia Routledge and Gene Wilder.

Garrett also firmly believed in bringing great names for us to listen admiringly to. They ranged from personal friends like John Gielgud to John Betjeman and from Benjamin Britten to Wedgewood Benn, from Peggy Ashcroft to Lord Hailsham, from John Arlott to Winston Churchill. One of these was quite unwittingly responsible for the most terrifying half hour I had spent thus far. He called me out and said;

'David, Sir Donald Wolfit is waiting in my study. Go and keep him company would you?'

Almost paralysed with stage fright I opened the door. The Great Actor was waiting patiently. He gave me a none too encouraging glance, and in an access of inarticulateness I seem to recall burbling away idiotically about the convex mirror on the wall. His great role was King Lear, and he must have decided that I was the nearest thing to the Fool that Garrett could provide.

Garrett's own favourite story was of writing to Evelyn Waugh and asking him to visit school. When he received a sarcastic response from Waugh saying that he would as well invite the whole Sixth form to visit him at Piers Court, Garrett pounced and wrote back thanking him profusely for his kind invitation, hired a coach and took thirty boys there.

'He rose to the occasion magnificently' said Garrett, 'and entertained us all in a most civilized fashion.'

For a picture of Garrett moving on his purposeful peregrinations about the school, I can hardly do better than quote Paul Vaughan in "Something in Linoleum."

"Nowadays probably his homosexuality would be obvious, but to us innocents it was not. All we knew was that he walked like a bit of a cissy; chin up, arms loose at his sides but hands turned outwards, wagging his shoulders with quick, alert steps, his approach often advertised by that peremptory, barking, upper class voice with its italicized rhythms."

The vignette is brilliantly incised, but I fancy he must have mellowed somewhat in the more historic environs of Bristol Grammar School. The same might account for what appears to have been a lower incidence of corporal punishment. I can recall only one boy being beaten at this time, though a friend, himself a victim, assures me there were many more. He tells me that the caning was administered by the School Sergeant, with Garrett an interested spectator. There was however a perhaps more pernicious form of punishment known as a "Prefects' Beating." This was carried out after a peremptory Prefects' "Trial" and the alleged offender was beaten with an old Plimsoll. Ironically enough on the one occasion when I was present (as a Prefect, not a victim), the punishment was carried out by my friend Austin. He of the white plimsolls at Dr. Bell's school, Fishponds.

There can be no question of Garrett's devotion to the long term interests of his pupils, although Peter Nichols in his autobiography, condemns him as being only interested in the Sixth Form and contemptuous of juniors. "Their behaviour is execrable," he said.

In his dealings with staff, he promoted the good and rapidly interred the bad. One incident produced pure drama. A notorious maths teacher was given to fearsome outbreaks of verbal violence (is it always a maths teacher?) I saw one boy, made to stand in front of class, who fainted clean away. All lived in fear of him, except one muscular young man who later became a well known BBC actor. As the angry master moved to hover over him, he simply stood up and delivered a perfect right hook to the face. The wounded teacher, blood pouring from his nose, staggered out and ran down the corridor to the Head's study, crying for vengeance and instant sacking. But it was the teacher, not the boy whom we never saw again. Garrett's comment was 'No teacher who reduces a boy to that level deserves a place on my staff'.

I personally however managed to provoke a situation in which he backed master against boy. We were almost without exception expected to join the "Officer's" (later "Junior") Training Corps. At the end of a year or so of parading and "field days", we were given, if proficient, a "Certificate A", after an interview by some superannuated Lieutenant. I was last one in, which surprised me because my of my initial. He failed me. I have no explanation other than some kind of racialism, which, though not common, was by no means non-existent. In view of that I decided that the time was better spent on my Spanish studies for HSC, rather that the Corps, so I went to the Master in charge and told him I was resigning. He was utterly horrified. 'You can't do that Datta!' he cried 'You can't do it.' But I did, and handed in my uniform. He had his revenge however. Each year there was a School shooting championship to win a magnificent solid silver Challenge Cup. Long hours at home with my Webley had shown me I could hit almost anything, still or moving. So I entered, and won. My score with the Lee Enfield. 22's was 59 out of 60.

But I never got the cup. J.C.Woods the master in charge ruled me ineligible because I had resigned from his precious Corps. Rather crossly I went to see the Headmaster claiming that the championship was a school event, not a JTC event.

Garrett knew the value of a master who spent every single spare minute of his time running the all important cadet force. Unhesitatingly, he ruled in his favour. But at least "Jesse" Woods knew who the best shot in the school was; and so did the chap who got the cup.

There was one sphere where Garrett was occasionally to be seen, but Beecroft never; that of the school playing field. Its importance could never be denied in any establishment that aspired to public school status; every teacher knew where the battle of Waterloo had been won; even scientists knew the meaning of "mens sana in corpore sano." Two men dominated this world; A.B.Carter (Junior English and cricket), and Mr. Gethins (French classics and Rugby). Early on, Carter picked out a rangy young teenager who had a good eye for the ball and elegant footwork at the crease. He felt he could make something of him.

He spent spent hour upon hour with him at the nets and fielding practice. His faith and tenacity were vindicated. The boy's name was Tom Graveney, and he went on to become Captain of England, and the nation's saviour in several grimly fought Test matches against Australia. On one occasion it fell to me to confront all six foot three of him in an end of term boxing match. Although I pursued him for all three rounds, Tom was awarded the verdict. He was already the school sports hero, and no gym master who valued his job could do other than award him the verdict. At least that was my "we wuz robbed" rationale. Tom was noble enough to remind me of the occasion when I met up with him in the Kings Arms, in Oxford many years later.

'I had a lot of fights when I was in the Commandos' he said. 'But never one as tough as that.'

That was good enough for me.

It was Rugby that I grew most keen on. Gethins turned us into a team that swept aside most opposition. My friend Austin Davis was a solid fullback and I a not very fast wing threequarter who was later turned into a left centre ("A useful swerve" the report said). It has to be accepted that there is something about the game of Rugby that those who have played it can never put aside. The schoolboy version was manly without being violent, and not nearly as painful as it looks to spectators. Besides, my brother had been something of a rising star, before being called to meet Rommel, and I tried to keep up the inheritance.

One day Garrett stopped me in school and said,

'David I was at the match yesterday and I was delighted to see you playing. I never had you figured for a rugger tough.'

But I wasn't unique. The best fast bowler in the cricket team was a six foot four aesthete called Denbury who read Auden and Isherwood and painted in the style of Modigliani. He went on to read

Frequent winners. BGS 1st XV
Including Tom Graveney and Bob McEwen

English at Downing. But my favourite school cricketer was a solid opening bat called Ron Alley. He left to read the history of Art and eventually became Curator of the Moderns at the Tate Gallery. It did my prestige no end of good to be able to take a friend to the Tate and show that I was well acquainted with the man who had "discovered" David Hockney and written the Gallery's official book on modern art.

But there was an less desirable element to school sports; a distinct element of snobbery. Clifton College would never give us a fixture, and that was not because they knew we could beat them hollow. Their social milieu was Eton and Harrow and Winchester so that we had to content ourselves with playing local High schools or less "classy" public schools. The whole ethos of the British public school system is immortalised in the now infamous poem, "Play up and play the game."

"The sand of the desert is sodden red
Red with the wreck of the square that broke.
The Gatling's jammed and the colonel's dead
........but the voice of a school boy rallied the ranks
'Play up, and play the game'"

With all its connotations of mowing down the Fuzzy Wuzzies
and slaughtering the Zulus, we Old Bristolians may feel relieved
that it was not one of our lot who perpetrated it. Sir Henry Newbold
the poet was an Old Cliftonian. We all know where the battle of
Waterloo was won; perhaps we can say something similar about
Omdurman and other triumphs of Empire.

One of the most impressive boys in my year was G.H.H.
Lambert. He was a Rugby forward, and wielded the Mace in the
OTC marching band. He was one of the front row wits in Beecroft's
classes, and though his academic abilities were strictly limited,
Garrett once said of him,

'That chap has more personality in his little finger than the lot
of you put together.'

It was Lambert who summed up Beecroft perfectly.

'I somehow made it into Cambridge' he told me years later 'But
I never met anyone to compare with Beecroft. If I go back to school
and meet him he still makes me feel like a clod hopping idiot.'

I had to confess myself saddened when I found that Lambert
gave vent to extreme expressions of traditional Imperialist sentiment,
particularly concerning people. Many years later I met an ex girl
friend of his who told me a long, complex story with a Caribbean
twist, which might well have had some bearing on the subject.

***

Inevitably, racialism became a prime subject of study, and
my own conclusions are somewhat bleak. I believe prejudice to
be universal among nations and in all continents in spite of noble

efforts at politcal correctness. It exists in host nations towards immigrants and among immigrants towards later arrivals. It was there when the New York Irish refused to fight for the North, and when the Australians tried to make the Aborigines disappear through interbreeding. In India it is enshrined in the Caste system and the laws of Manu promulgate fearsome penalties for offenders.

My experience has been made tolerable by a simple rationalisation. I believe the proponents of race prejudce fall into two categories, which I call "tacit" and "obsessional". The former I find bearable. Most of the time it is barely noticeable, except among the hypersensitive. Life goes on, friends stay friends. But the obsessive form is a different matter. Those infected by it have an overwhelming urge to talk and argue and "joke" about race at every opportunity. Trashy comedians build whole careers on it. The politically minded join violent parties of the far right. Thugs spend Saturday nights looking for lone immigrants to beat to death.

I am only too relieved to report that among the fundamentally easy going British, the "tacit" numerically far exceed the "obsessional".

We learned how to stook a cornfield.

Chapter 14

By the spring of 1944, Churchill's remark about "the beginning of the end" seemed to be justified. The Russians, equipped with better tanks and guns, had recovered the Ukraine and were pushing the Germans back, although with tremendous losses on both sides, across Poland. Bomber Command and the USAAF were bringing death and destruction to all German cities, and they themselves were suffering terrible casualties. In Italy my brother was free of the unpleasantness of the last ditch German defence and was moving up towards Florence. As one of the first to enter the city of the Medici, he would soon find himself sitting with the Mayor on the Ponte Vecchio, discussing local health matters, and drinking a well earned cognac.

In the jungles of Burma his brother-in-law Len Robson was not quite so lucky; but that justly famed Bristolian (and friend of his wife) General Slim was beginning to show the Japanese the way home from the borders of India. In the Pacific the Americans had taken Guadalcanal and were intent on making good MacArthur's pledge, "I shall return" to the Philippines, en-route for Japan itself.

And then, on June 6th, came D-Day.

Left wingers had been agitating for it for over a year. Their posters all over the country called on the Churchill government to "Open a Second Front Now". Their suspicion was that the Western powers were quite happy to let the Russians exhaust themselves pushing the Germans back; and that we would only invade if Stalin looked like conquering Germany on his own. Churchill and Eisenhower, however, knew they dared not risk another Dunkirk, and waited until their strength was overwhelming and the weather was right.

In fact when it happened the greatest invasion the world had ever seen, passed almost unnoticed in most of the British Isles. Censorship made sure that only if success were certain, we could all be told about it. One hundred and fifty thousand men in four thousand ships, supported by many hundreds of planes landed on five French beaches and fought their way ashore. It was the event all Europe had awaited for five long years. The hardest time of all was had by the Americans on Omaha beach, where their tank landing craft failed and they suffered over 2,000 casualties. Once ashore, once the beachhead was established, the BBC broke the news. There would be many months of hard fighting ahead, and a worrying German counter attack, but at long last we could begin to feel that victory was a probability, not a mere possibility.

At home the prospect of peace suddenly seemed to galvanise the Labour Party into action. Until then an amicable Coalition with the Conservatives under Churchill had directed the nation's destiny. With the Russians advancing so fast, the Labour Party too now needed to establish its credentials with people who might soon be asked to vote in an election.

My father's party work had increased to a high rate. Known throughout the city for chairing meetings, addressing party rallies, and even judging 'baby shows', his photograph frequently appeared in the local paper chatting to people like Stafford Cripps. He had also begun to establish a name in far left circles as a political analyst, and wrote an excellent article on the U.S. Presidential election in which Governor Dewey was taking on Roosevelt. He correctly forecast that F.D.R.'s 'New Deal' policies had won him enough Union support to beat Dewey whose fame rested mainly on his 'racket busting'.

The article appeared, as did several others, in a publication called 'Labour Monthly', edited by the secretary of the Communist Party, Palme Dutt. Later to become vilified as an unrepentant Stalinist, Palme Dutt nevertheless wrote what to me was the finest ever social and economic analysis of India, called 'India To-day'. It made thousands of converts to Indian Independence and greatly helped the work of Krishna Menon's India League.

At this point I have to admit to a reading list that would in popular parlance be termed schizophrenic. I read many of my father's books in the Gollancz series like Upton Sinclair's famous work on Chicago, "The Jungle". I tried to develop my social conscience with "The Ragged Trouser'd Philanthropist," and I even wrestled with "Ten

Days that Shook the World". I read Hewlett Johnson's "Socialist Sixth of the World" which made me feel that if a great Christian like the Dean of Canterbury could praise Russia, then Stalin must be O.K. I also read P.G. Wodehouse and some Evelyn Waugh; but my steady diet was one of the monthly magazines 'Aeroplane' or 'Flight'. My urge to get into the cockpit of a Spitfire had never diminished; every night I would drop off to sleep, soothed by the imagined roar of Rolls Royce Merlin engines, and I, and a friend called Terry were remarkably good at aircraft recognition, and could rattle off the statistics of cruising speeds, bomb loads, and armaments of almost all allied and enemy warplanes.

This intellectual dichotomy of mine produced two critical situations. John Garrett had endowed a Poetry Prize at school. Three of us entered it and, presumably because our work was equally bad, he divided the prize between all three entrants. For my prize I chose a book called 'Aircraft of the Fighting Powers'. The English master whose job it was to arrange the prize giving came to me with a worried expression. 'I really don't know if this would be a suitable prize', he said pompously, 'But I will ask the headmaster'. J.G's response was characteristically progressive. 'Give the boy what he wants.'

However it was not the aircraft recognition factor so much as the passion I developed for George Formby, his films and his 'banjulele' playing, that finally made my father feel action needed to be taken. He responded to an invitation from J.G. to all senior boys' parents to come in and discuss their progress.

'Headmaster, I'm really quite worried,' he said, 'all David wants to do when he leaves school is become an airline pilot.' Garrett gave an indulgent laugh and said,

'Please don't worry Dr.Datta, he'll grow out of it. After all it's just the modern version of wanting to be an engine driver. And I don't know much about this George Formby chappy, but we must remember that even William Shakespeare loved to have his clowns'

By then my father had become elected Chairman of the Bristol Borough Labour Party. He was also President of the Trades Council, a sort of local T.U.C. The agent Ted Rees was deeply grateful to him for his skill and dedication, which even included addressing many open air meetings.

'Homes fit for heroes' was high on the agenda, as were all the promises of the Beveridge report for a lifetime's security. There was to be a National Labour Party Conference later in the year at which all these matters would be thrashed out. Because the Labour Party (in those days at least) prided itself on its regard for democracy, resolutions would be passed which the executive had the bounden duty to incorporate into its manifesto. This would be put in front of the electors when the first post war elections came, and the people, if they voted Labour, would secure the future they wanted for their children.

Ted Rees decided that my father should be rewarded for all his years of hard work on the Party's behalf, and he proposed that my father should be Bristol's delegate to the National Party Conference. This gave him a strong voice in the choice of resolution that would be put forward; and all who knew him meant this would be on the subject above all others; Independence for India. India had become a matter of prime concern for the government. When the Japanese had reached the borders of India, Gandhi had declared a Civil Disobedience Movement. At the same time many prisoners had joined the Indian National Army to fight with them. In 1942 Sir Stafford Cripps had been sent out with a special mission to offer India 'Dominion Status'. This had been flatly rejected, and in 1942, Civil Disobedience had been stepped up. The British responded by banning Congress and imprisoning Gandhi, Nehru and other leaders. The result was nationwide violence and leaderless riots in which there were 60,000 arrests and many deaths.

To anyone supporting the British War effort this became something of an embarrassment. It was about this time that my father's friend Alderman Burgess, now Lord Mayor, invited us to dinner at the Mansion House. During the evening he showed us the City Treasures which included the famous Bristol Gold Plate, about 18 inches in diameter. It transpired that during the Bristol Reform Bill Riots of 1832, the Bishop's Palace had been burned down, the Mansion House sacked, and the Gold Plate seized. It had been cut into several hundred pieces and distributed among the crowd. When the unrest was over the City authorities set about 'buying back' every single piece of gold and welding them together to restore the piece to its original splendour.

It was a neat reminder that it wasn't just the Indians who rioted, the British had shown themselves capable of doing so to. But there was a further lesson. The restoration of the plate, like the Restoration of the Monarchy after the Civil War, demonstrated how deep rooted is British dedication to all forms of tradition. Change is merely a temporary aberration.

Thus it was decided that the Labour Party's motion at the National Conference was to be in favour of complete Independence for India. I did happen to overhear one conversation at a meeting in which a local member asked Ted Rees if there were not other subjects they should be promoting. But the agent was a strong character and he knew my father's value.

'We'll get this out of the way,' he said, 'Then at next year's conference you can put your ideas forward.'

***

The Conference took place at Central Hall, Westminister on December 11th, 1944. Harold Laski was elected Chairman. The Executive included Attlee, Ellen Wilkinson, Arthur Greenwood, Aneurin Bevan, Ernest Bevin, Hugh Dalton, Herbert Morrison, Edith Summerskill, and indeed the full panoply of Labour stars who would come to rule the country within a matter of months. During five years of war, those leaders had subdued their reforming instincts to follow a government of National Unity led by Winston Churchill, until Germans and Japanese would be defeated. Attlee, Bevin and Cripps had held ministerial posts and acquitted themselves well in the war effort. But now peace was on the horizon and voices on the left were calling for a better future for the servicemen who would soon be returning. The most important document in all their thinking was the Beveridge Report, a non party plan which had been produced in 1942. This looked towards a Britain with a National Health Service, a national insurance scheme, improved education, and security 'from the cradle to the grave.' Labour leaders were expected to make this the basis for their manifesto in fighting the first General Election to be held in ten years.

It happened that in spite of such a unity of purpose, two key members of the executive were seen to sit well apart from each other. Ernest Bevin, the bluff no -nonsense countryman from Somerset, had developed a certain distaste for Herbert Morrison, the smooth quick thinking Londoner. The situation gave rise to a remark that passed into the annals of Labour history. When a third person was trying to ameliorate matters he said to Bevin,

'The trouble with Herbert, he's his own worst enemy.' Ernie's reply came galloping back; 'Not so long as I'm alive he ain't.'

The conference began with 'keynote' speeches about the end of coalition government and expressions of confidence in a forthcoming Labour victory. They included enthusiastic forecasts of rent restrictions, and new housing plans, and the action to be taken about a soon to be defeated Germany, and Greece, which seemed to be heading for civil war.

On the afternoon of the third day Jim Griffiths spoke at length about social insurance, workmen's compensation, and the health service. The latter led to a resolution in favour of a Nationally funded service, after a detailed speech by Dr. Stark Murray of the Socialist Medical Association.

My father rose to second this motion. Typically he expressed due deference to the previous speaker as "a Professor of Medicine" and found him inspirational. He spoke quite briefly, but won full attention from the floor; most of the delegates at such a time would have been intrigued by a contribution on home issues by a doctor who was an Indian; in fact he was almost certainly the first delegate of colonial origin since the days of Saklatvala.

The fourth day was memorable for speeches by two heroes of the left 'Manny' Shinwell and Ian Mikardo who called for unqualified economic controls,   public ownership of the means of production, land, buildings, heavy industry, banks, transport and coal. It was an awesome sounding list, that would dominate the next decade, and, as many feared, put Britain well on the way to becoming a Socialist Republic.

My father's moment in history came on the morning of the last day of the Conference. The subject on the agenda was India, and the motion to be proposed called for full Independence instead of the 'Dominion Status' that had already been rejected by the Congress Party, resulting in strikes, riots and many jail sentences. Rather wisely the motion was proposed by a delegate from the N.U.R. called C.W. Bridges; somehow it carried more of a feeling of commitment, if it came from some one more detached than my father. It was a sound speech, wholly anti-imperialist, and called for the release of all political prisoners, and the re-opening of negotiations for setting up a national government.

My father rose to second the motion and was at once recognised for his previous contribution on the need for a National Health Service.   But this time he spoke with a power few other delegates could equal. Singing lessons had given him all he needed to know about breathing, pitch and voice projection. It was the culmination of many years of political campaigning, in draughty halls, and open air gatherings, and he knew he had to strive to emulate Keir Hardie or even Edmund Burke.

The audience responded to his passion, as if they had been treated to a moment of pure theatre, and he ended with an unashamed peroration, calling on the executive committee to end their procrastination and give his country its freedom.   He said:

'The Chairman has said "India is a vast prison house, and the key to that prison house is in Downing Street." I will make just this modification. Today when Labour stands at the threshold of power, the key to the unlocking of that prison house is on the floor of this Conference.

'You should take up that magic key. You have the power to unlock those gates.'

The applause from the floor was nothing less than an ovation. This unique delegate with his perfect diction and total conviction had given them a lesson in oratory, and in so doing reminded them all of what power they possessed.

Needless to say there was a counter attack. Attlee and the Labour Executive were still members of a government led by Winston Churchill. If they were to release the Indian leaders and promise Independence they would be held guilty of virtually wrecking the Empire while the war was still being fought.

A man called James Walker rose to attack my father's motion on behalf of the Executive. He argued against any notion of Indian Independence and in favour of 'continued negotiations' towards the goal of 'Dominion Status' which had already been rejected by Gandhi and Nehru, and was the reason why they had been imprisoned.

The Walker resolution failed dismally. The 'Independence' resolution proposed by Bridges and supported so powerfully by my father, with support from Reverend Sorensen and others, was the one the delegates wanted. They passed it 'with acclamation'.

The next day the News Chronicle gave my father front page headlines. Ian MacKay saw the day as a revolt by from the floor by ordinary members against an over cautious executive.

He picked out my father's speech as the most dramatic moment of the entire week long conference.

Ordinary members from all over Britain had taken the vital step that within months of the war's ending would lead to the Mountbatten mission and the end of 300 years of British rule, culminating in

Nehru's famous speech about the "midnight hour."

The 1944 Labour Party Conference was perhaps the most significant conference in the entire history of British politics. The decisions taken there changed the whole structure of the nation for up to half a century. Mines, railways, heavy industry were taken into public ownership: rigid controls were imposed on finance. A unique Welfare State was created with Health and Welfare benefits for the entire population. Those changes remained in place until the advent of a strange concatenation of the micro chip, Margaret Thatcher, Arthur Scargill and Red Robbo forty years later, and even then most of the principles that had been established continued in place.

My father had played a small but vital role in those changes. He returned to Bristol simply aware that he had had a great privilege in taking part in the British democratic process. He had been born into an Imperial society where notions of freedom were viewed with the utmost suspicion. Yet here in the country of his adoption, the ideas that motivated men and women at all levels were the precise opposite. It was a contradiction that had persisted throughout British history. But now at last the values of Mill and Bentham and Thomas Paine were in the ascendant. The maps of the world were about to be re-drawn. The British Empire would soon become a subject for Professors of History and Romantic film makers.

The triumphant Independence chapter must not be closed without an admission of the dreadful conflicts that took place in the sub-continent after 1946. Under Mountbatten's chairmanship, Jinnah's Moslem League won its battle for an independent Pakistan. A British civil servant spent all of a week drawing up the border line. The result was refugees by the million, bloody massacres, a legacy of conflict that led to full scale wars in the fifties and seventies, and a violent conflict over Kashmir that remains unresolved.

In the decade that followed Indian Independence, most British Colonies and Protectorates made their bids for Home Rule. In some, like Singapore and the British West Indies, the processes were relatively free from violence. In others, bitter conflicts arose. Many of my school friends were conscripted to take up arms and fight against what the British establishment saw as communist inspired movements in places as disparate as Cyprus and Malaysia, where so called "Communist Bandits" fought to seize power. The conflict here amounted to an all British dress rehearsal for the awfulness that the Americans would one day inflict on Viet Nam. Savage repression also took place in Kenya as the British Colonial Office strove to cling to power, while in Rhodesia, a different battle ensued as white settlers led by Ian Smith tried to hijack the Independence movement.

There would be one area above all where the last gasp of the British Empire would be heard and seen by the whole world. In 1956 Prime Minister Anthony Eden, Winston Churchill's political heir, concocted a devious plan to invade Egypt and prevent Nasser, its new republican President, from nationalising the gateway to Empire, the Suez canal. The rest of the world raised its hands in horror as British troops, aided by the French and the Israelis, landed in strength and bombed and shelled their way towards Cairo.

It seemed this was the way the Empire would end; with both bangs and whimpers. The escapade would be called off, thanks to world pressure and the intervention of the Americans, who were still at that point in time, able to act with a sense of political rectitude. Half a century on many are tempted to pronounce on the desirability or otherwise on some of the regimes that have replaced Imperial control. It is easy to point to Zimbabwe and Burma with "I told you so" fingers.

But few would dare to deny the moral right of any subject nation to self determination, or the right to learn from its own mistakes, however long and painful the process may be.

My father was instrumental in winning that right for his own country; and for helping to create the first National Health Service in the country of his adoption.

Chapter 15

In the whole of the 20th Century there can hardly have been a more momentous year than 1945. The Pacific witnessed the greatest Naval battles in history from Leyte to the landing on Japanese soil at Okinawa. The Americans also grudgingly allowed the Royal Navy to take part too, sending what became known as the 'Forgotten Fleet'. In this Lt. Douglas Boyd flew an Avenger, one of his crew was killed, and he was awarded the D.S.C. Eventually he returned to Bristol and married my friend June.

In Berlin, the mass murderer Hitler committed suicide and in August the Americans dropped atomic bombs on Hiroshima and Nagasaki, killing over a hundred thousand people and setting the markers for the Cold War that would dominate the world for the next half century and beyond.

May 8th was dedicated as VE Day. Throughout the land, the British who had had little to celebrate for 6 years, organised street parties and bonfires. Trafalgar Square was packed with a bibulous multitude, and Winston Churchill the nation's hero, waved his cigar and gave his famous "V" sign from Buckingham Palace. Even the little "Green" opposite Snowdon House was given over to a bonfire, and much cavorting with bottles, and my rugby chum Austin Davis and I performed our favourite party piece duet, the music hall song "A mother was bathing her baby one night..."

And then there followed something as close to Revolution as British history could get. In the 1945 General Election the nation turned its back on both Churchill and the Empire, voting for fairness and equality of opportunity, leaving only the diehards to cling on in Malaya, and Suez for several more years, until Eisenhower put a stop to it.

My father had made such an impact at the Party Conference, that the agent pressed him to stand as an M.P. The vacant constituency was Bridgewater. Nothing would have delighted him more that to follow in the footsteps of Saklatvala, but after long agonising he regretfully turned the offer down. Bridgewater was a small industrial town surrounded by the green fields of Somerset, and the Quantock Hills where the Squires still ruled, and hunted deer with hounds. He was above all else, devoted to his family and he felt he dared not take the risk in middle age of abandoning a secure job for one which, however historic, might put our futures in jeopardy.

The election was nevertheless supremely exciting for the family and my father was in demand all over Bristol for speeches and rallies. The biggest of these was held in the Colston Hall which was filled to capacity to hear Harold Laski, the National Party Chairman. He spoke in the usual academic way (he was head of L.S.E.) making sound dialectical points in an almost confidential manner. Then my father stood up to give the vote of thanks. I had never before heard him speak in public and was astounded. If Caruso had been a politician he could not have made a speech of more sustained, ringing tones. We at the back heard every word, and the audience was galvanised. At the very least their local man had shown the big cheese from London how to make a speech. My brother's wife and I looked at each other as though we had heard a revelation from the mountain tops.

I was introduced to Laski. He asked politely what I would do when I left school. This was no time to talk of airline pilots; I thought quickly and said I would probably read law.
'Go to America my boy' he said, 'America's the place to read law.' He sounded a bit like W.C. Fields, but he was a kindly man and a great name in his day.

I teamed up with Austin, and we made nuisances of ourselves at several Conservative Party meetings. The one at Fishponds Church Hall proved memorable. The candidate was a Captain Britton, later famous for TuF Shoes. He was standing in for the previous M.P. Captain Bernays who had been killed in the War. But we found this no occasion for false sympathies. We heckled steadily throughout, and when the Chairman called for questions. Austin rose to his feet. He of the white plimsolls at Dr. Bell's School, had by now become a promising classicist. He had also just won the School prize for oratory. The subject, set by Langford, was Cato calling on the Senate to send an army to destroy Hannibal of Carthage. ("Delenda est Carthago") With that under his belt, Austin would have regarded a village hall audience as a pushover. He had decided on being a Liberal and he rose to ask a question about Conservative agricultural policy, which quite astonished me, since he had no farming connections or particular interest in that direction. But it was a wonderful opportunity for a speech and Austin began to make it. After several minutes of rising cadences and sound rhetorical tricks the Chairman took fright and made a naive mistake.

'You're supposed to ask questions,' he cried, 'not make speeches. This is the place for speeches!' He indicated the rostrum. Austin at once said,

'Ah, thank you very much Sir,' and moved purposefully towards the platform steps. As a man, the committee members rose and surged forward to head him off.

'This meeting is now closed!' called the chairman desperately, as the hall broke up amid laughter and confusion. The staid conservatives of Fishponds were shocked at our revolutionary behaviour and lack of respect for Mr. Churchill's loyal and even heroic followers. It was as if the Paris mob had broken in. But the same was happening all over the country. Coldrick, the Labour man won the seat by a large majority.

It is hard for anyone of the Television generation to understand what a combination of trauma and mystery a General Election offered in those days, particularly since nothing like it had occurred for ten years. To-day a General Election is a Media Event, with its minute by minute results, breathlessly excited commentaries, its 'swingometers' and its graphic explanations. It has more in common with 'Saturday Night at the London Palladium', than the world of serious political thinking. People vote unashamedly for the celebrities of their choice, and any connection with democracy seems purely fortuitous. Parties steal each others' policies with impunity.

On that day all that the many hundreds of labour supporters could do was to gather in the Drill Hall in Bristol and wait in a state of high neurosis for words that would come by radio or telephone. I re-call a breathless party agent rushing to the instrument every few minutes, then back to my father and his committee to report a win or a loss. The nervous tension went on for hours, candidates not knowing whether they would become powers in the land or nonentities.

And then, as I recall an excited Ted Rees hung up the telephone and rushed over to our group.

'I've just been talking to Herbert Morrison,' he panted. 'He says it's a landslide! A landslide. We're winning hundreds of seats!'
The smiles that greeted him were of Cheshire cat proportions, and the word 'landslide' dominated the hubbub in the Hall So that was it. The King would summon Mr. Attlee and ask him to form a Labour Government. Ellen Wilkinson could begin to agonise over education. The miners would tell the world that 'they were the bosses now.' Nye Bevan could plan his battle with the Doctors. Ernest Bevin could start to try and understand Zionism. And Stafford Cripps would look with horror at the Treasury balance sheets and realise that his party had inherited a bankrupt State, that rationing would have to be brought back, and ordinary people would almost be fighting for a bucket of coal. Things were so bad that the great economic Guru Maynard Keynes would be sent to America to ask for more time to pay off our debts, and even ask to borrow more dollars.
In many ways we would be worse fed than during the war, thanks to American supplies of flour, dried egg, corned beef and Spam. And we still had long to wait before the return to our tables of that profound symbol of normality, the banana. When it finally happened, the first boat from Jamaica into Bristol was deemed worthy of a civic ceremony; the Lord Mayor and his attendants in Top Hats and Tails stood on the quay to welcome the Captain and his

Bananas are back! A civic reception for the first boatload
(Photo courtesy of Bristol United Press)

precious cargo.

Auberon Waugh records how, at Piers Court, he stared in amazement at these strange yellow fruits on the breakfast table; then father Evelyn arrived, seized them both and ate them in an access of ravenous lust.

***

The first election in 6 years brought a nation-wide flurry of activity and interest in politics, so that normally quiescent people would find themselves going to meetings, and joining in debates, writing to the papers.

One man who could not resist entering the general fray was the headmaster of Bristol Grammar School. In his youth, along with his friends like Auden and Spender, he had affected leftish sympathies. But now he was in a position of power and responsibility leading a privately funded school, four hundred years old, and founded by people who had known Henry VIII. Silence might have been golden, but the Bristol Labour Party was in such a position of power that threats were being issued in all directions, even at the very existence of public and grammar schools.

A key man in all this was a large gent of Liverpudlian persuasion called Alderman Harry Hennessy. I have a photograph of him marching next to my father through Queen Square, Union banner flying high. Harry and others made speeches threatening all private schools with closure. Garret could not ignore the challenge. In a widely reported speech he deplored the threat to great schools being made by people who were themselves "virtually illiterate."

The shaft struck home. The Alderman was perhaps justifiably furious. This was a personal insult; it meant a duel to the death.

The first my father got to know of it was an anxious call from agent Rees. They met to discuss the matter.

'He's going to sue,' said Ted. 'He's going to sue for slander. He's already been to see his solicitor.'

They discussed the legalities of the situation, the courses of action open, and whether it might just 'blow over'. Ted thought not.

'Never seen him so hopping mad,' he said, 'he wants Garrett's guts for garters.'

Then a thought occurred to him.

'You've got a boy at the school, haven't you?' he asked. 'Is there any possibility you could go to the school, see Garrett, and talk things over?'

My father agreed, it just might do some good.

And so there was a meeting. The Chairman of the Party, my Dad, telephoned my Headmaster, John Garrett, and arranged to come in and see him. 'At your very earliest convenience, please, Headmaster.'

Many a father has had to go and meet many a headmaster over some problem with a pupil. But this was no case of George

Formby adulation. This surely must have been the first time where a father has had to go and speak severely to a headmaster because of a problem caused by the headmaster himself. Sadly I have no verbatim report from either side on what took place at the meeting, but I am irresistibly reminded of the most famous of poems by the great Poet of Empire, Rudyard Kipling;

"East is East and West and West is West
And never the twain shall meet
But there is neither East nor West
Border, nor Breed nor Birth,
When two strong men stand face to face
Though they come from the ends of the earth."

It would hardly have occurred to Kipling, nurtured on Imperial conquest, (the man who sent his own son to die in the trenches), that two strong men might succeed in finding a different way to resolve their problems. These two strong men possessed such charisma that the air between them would have been utterly filled with pure, undiluted charm. Charm enough to bring down Empires, leave alone satisfy local Labour Party campaigners.

My father went away with the promise of a full and personal apology to the offended politician. It must have been in the form of a letter, written in Garrett's neat hand, with some beautifully chosen phrases. As a friend of Auden's and co-anthologist of "The Poet's Tongue" he would have known which ones to use.

Harry Hennessy was not the kind of man to frame it and put it on his wall. He accepted it, and then set about the tasks of bulldozing a lot of eighteenth century buildings, and surrounding Bristol, in all its loveliest spots, with housing estates for the families of the returning heroes.

News CHRONICLE, Saturday, December 16, 1944

LABOUR DEMANDS RELEASE OF INDIAN LEADERS

"Key to unlock prison gates is on floor of conference"

By IAN MACKAY

ALMOST unanimously and in defiance of their national leaders the rank and file of the Labour Party at the closing session of their annual conference in London yesterday carried a strong resolution demanding the release of Nehru and the other imprisoned Indian political leaders.

They urged "the immediate ending of the political deadlock by negotiations with all leaders of the Indian people, with a view to the formation of a responsible national government which will rally the entire population of India to the anti-Fascist cause."

This proposal, put forward by the Railwaymen, was strongly resisted by the Executive, whose spokesman, Mr. James Walker, M.P.—for some reason which he did not make clear to the conference—declared that if it was carried the British would have to quit India tomorrow.

On deaf ears

He laid great stress on the greatness of the Japanese menace in the East, and declared that not one of the Allied nations—not even Russia—wanted Britain to leave India before the Japanese were defeated.

His appeal fell on deaf ears, however, and the resolution was overwhelmingly carried on a show of hands.

The big moment of the debate came when an Indian delegate, Mr. D. Dhuria, who is chairman of the Bristol Labour Party, went to the rostrum and declared, amid prolonged cheers, that India, if not given her freedom, would be lured in a night from being a silent subordinate into a willing ally.

Angry scene

Joad enlivens a debate

In one man's hands

Harrow and Eton

Agriculture

Education

SANTA CLAUS IS A CORPORAL

The Army Post Office, overcoming the difficulties of floods, mud and smashed bridges, is now delivering your Christmas mail to the boys "over there." Corporal who is distributing parcels to men of a British corps in Holland. Picture below, also taken near the front in the West, shows soldiers buying toys to send home at a gift shop run for the troops.

Offensive in Arakan has opened

THE offensive to recapture the Arakan region of Southern Burma opened Thursday, said a cable reaching London last night.

Wine at 8s. 9d.

News Chronicle Headlines for my father's speech.

Chapter 16

There is no system better designed to produce people capable of ruling Empires than that of the British Public School with its overwhelming devotion to hierarchy. A child begins as a vulnerable nonentity aged eight or nine. and battles its way upwards through the class system until nine or eight years later he or she breasts the mountain top, and can gaze down serenely at those still roped together on the ledges below. By now he is a Sixth Former, and if sufficiently deserving in the eyes of authority, a Prefect, lording it over all he surveys. He has his examination milestones safely behind him and can prepare to gain entry into the University of his choice. If, as often happens this means Oxford or Cambridge, it is best achieved by winning one of the scholarships offered by those revered institutions. These were normally 'open' to competitive endeavour from all the nation's schools, or 'closed 'for the particular school concerned. A wealthy school like Clifton College had many 'closed' scholarships; Bristol Grammar School had rather few. Having achieved reasonably good results in Higher Schools Certificate a select number of us were thus invited to stay on for another year at school in order to work for such scholarships.

I had been made a 'Prefect' in the preceding year, a surprise promotion which speaks well for Garrett's administrative abilities. I had joined an allegedly forward thinking group of boys, which included the fast bowling aesthete, Denbury. and the multi-talented Brian Martin. We read the latest Faber publications of poets like Auden, MacNeice, Dylan Thomas, David Gascoyne and so on. There were similar groups of classicists and scientists. Our desired books often simply 'appeared', usually after the lunch hour, with no signs of receipts from George's bookshop. We also studied the lives of the French Post Impressionist Painters, with particular emphasis on their hatred of authority and Middle Class convention. At the age of rising seventeen, all such people were our heroes, and I was lured into writing a tract lampooning the Head of School. He of course got to read it, was most upset and reported me to the headmaster.

Far from disciplining me he took no action at all, and several months later I was delighted to be made a Prefect. Garrett was clearly following the principle that, faced with a disruptive tendency in a pupil, the best way to curb it is to give him status and responsibility. Not quite "to catch a thief " but equally effective.

Adolescence is at the best of times a disturbing, even dangerous affair, and for us complicated by many conflicting pressures. In our case there was the special aspect of being in a Public Day School in a major city, with lives to be led beyond the four walls. If manliness is largely a matter of the pursuit of the opposite sex, there were Saturday night hops all over town; and there were plenty of pretty girls to be met from the many girls' schools in town. If sex pulled one way, Rugby pulled the other, although Garrett quite keenly noted that the Rugger toughs were "always the most sexually advanced." Later I realised that he might not have been talking in exclusively heterosexual terms.

Perhaps the most overwhelming factor was to have reached the age when one could drink in the town's innumerable pubs, and those with indulgent car owning parents could pursue escapades far and wide. On one life enhancing Christmas, I was taught to drink deeper by a boy of more mature inclinations than most called R.P.J. Smith. He was also the team's scrum half. No position for the faint hearted that, where you are constantly at the feet of eight hefty forwards, seemingly intent on kicking you to death. Ray's father was a highly successful furniture dealer, and I always professionally admired his slogan - "Your pound is worth thirty shillings if spent at Smith's!" Ray was short, chunky and had very blonde hair. Once Garrett called out to him in the street, "Smith, what lovely hair you have !".This did not however prevent him from sentencing him to physical chastisement for "anti-social behaviour " on more than one occasion. It was Ray who approached me and suggested I join him and a friend, a most handsome boy called Rees, who looked like a young Clark Gable, in a 'booze up'.

'What on earth is that?' I asked naively. 'Well,' he explained, 'You've got a car, and we've got a car. We just get in them and drive to Weston-Super-Mare. We put a pound each in the kitty and we stop and have a drink at every pub on the way.'

I said it sounded like fun, and could I bring our fly half, Micky Malone.

That evening my social education reached degree level, as I learned the differences between bottled and draught beer, 'tots' of whisky and the various sickly liquids that people put into their gin. Suffice to say that I drove home, head spinning and crawled into bed. As I tried to sleep I became aware of insistent tapping noises in my head and was seized with panic. 'My God,' I thought, 'first time drinking, and I've got D.T's already, just like Modigliani.'

In fact the sound was not in my head, It came from the Death Watch Beetle in the Oak beams of Snowdon House. It was the beginning of the death sentence for the house, if not for me.

Next day, with a head like overboiled cabbage, I suddenly recalled that I had been picked to play Rugby for a kind of schoolboy trial for the Bristol Club. I made it to the ground. Fortunately I had been picked to play at Wing Threequarter. To my great relief the ball never came near me all afternoon. My friend June came to watch. She said afterwards that a man standing next to her had said he'd have liked to have seen "that Indian" get the ball. "That Indian" was highly relieved he didn't. And needless to say he was not invited to play for Bristol, as his brother had been.

Unlike generations of city youths to come we seemed to have little inclination towards violence. In some measure this may be attributable to the game of Rugby. Crowd violence is overwhelmingly a feature of Soccer, not Rugby matches. Nor is it a matter of class, because the Welsh are certainly not all middle class. Psychologists and sociologist might like to pick that thought up and run with it. Equally we lacked the same desperate attachment to guns that some modern youths have. We had just been through six years of war. We knew what really big bangs sounded like. Most of us had been taught to use a Lee Enfield or even a Sten gun. And many had lost relatives to German or Japanese marksmen. Joe Young was one of those; his "Para" brother never returned from Arnhem.

Echoes of war continued to reverberate. With my sister in law I went to Temple Meads to meet my brother, returning after two years absence in North Africa and Italy. He stepped from the train almost bulging out of his battledress, having gained two stones in weight. His smile of joyous greeting turned to astonishment at seeing me, a kid who was now almost a man. He and I would be exploring most of the Pubs in Bristol during the months to come; partly because he knew that I too would soon have to put on a uniform and leave my charmed existence behind. Like most men who have seen action he said almost nothing about his experiences, and then only after repeated prompting; in any case his main concern was to set up one of the new National Health medical practices, with his partner to be, Major Beddoe.

But one story was bound to emerge in time. With the First Army in Italy, he had been attached to the leading columns that were now pursuing the Germans, who were at long last retreating. They had moved into a position where there was a large ammunition dump, and he had started to set up his medical tent by a wall. On the other side there were some Engineers moving 88mm shells. Suddenly, there was a huge explosion. He ran round to see what had happened and found three men lying on the ground unconscious, their legs shattered. He took the only course possible. He and his orderlies got the men, one at a time, onto a table in the open air, and amputated all six of their legs one after the other. It took just twenty minutes "I never worked so hard in my life," was his comment. I asked what happened to them. "They all died," he said, "They were probably dead when I got to them."

If in later years my brother drank too well it may well have been to erase such memories, and if anyone chose to criticise him, I merely ask how they would have behaved in such a situation. I know many who would simply have cut and run. He himself was mentioned in dispatches, but he was never inclined to take his holidays in Italy.

My Sixth form coterie continued to put on the style and some of us even sat for University Scholarships. I took one for Queen's

College, Cambridge and travelled there to be interviewed. It was a sudden glimpse of reality in that I sensed that in fact I hadn't even begun the true process of education. The Cambridge Don was most charming and gave me a nice lecture on Forster's 'Passage To India'. Perhaps he was even one of his friends   Sadly though, he decided he didn't want me there. The scholarship was won by friend Joe Young, who took it in history and won a place at St. John's, Oxford. I had done tolerably well in "Higher Certificate", though no exam ever gave me the satisfaction I had achieved in School Certificate by getting a credit in Geography.

A question had come up on the railway systems of USA. and I answered it brilliantly by remembering the words of the song "Chatanooga Chu Chu"

"When you hear the whistle blowing eight to a bar
Then you know that Tennessee ain't very far"

We sat around in the Great Hall talking art, politics, Jazz, literature and what we thought was philosophy, and one of our number was a very pleasant and intelligent boy called Mervyn Paice. It was easy enough to get deferment from 'call-up' for educational reasons, but Mervyn decided that if one had to join the army for two years or even more, one might as well get it over and done with as soon as possible. His decision was to prove not merely fatal, but appallingly so. He left and joined the Army Education Corps. Within a few months he was posted to what was still the British Protectorate of Palestine. No one heard from him, but all heard about him. It was to become my generation's first horror story.

One of the favoured little drinking dens in central Bristol was a cellar bar in Queen's Road called 'the Dugout'. The place acquired a certain infamy. One lunch hour the Senior Classics master, Langford, watched Joe Young remove his school cap and dive down the steps. Intrigued he followed and saw him ordering his shandy at the bar. The incident was reported to Garrett. Joe, previously

'Second Prefect', was reduced to the ranks.

But far more serious matters were afoot in the Dugout. At Prep school one had known a character called 'Ticky' (T.K.) Daniels, whose father was a sea captain. We had been shown around the vessel. Daniels appeared to have fallen by the wayside scholastically; but we heard of him in a far more sinister context. 'The Downs' was Bristol's spacious area of unspoilt parkland, close to the Suspension bridge, and one spot had always been used by public speakers. It now transpired that a group of thinly disguised fascists who used the Dugout as their base, were regularly making speeches on the Downs, and one of their key performers was T.K. Daniels. After the war we had just fought, with images of concentration camp horrors freshly brought to our cinema screens, it was hard to believe that people could be so diabolically possessed by anti-semitism that they were prepared to preach their doctrines as though nothing evil had occurred. The leading speaker was a man called Webster, and his hero was Oswald Moseley who, astonishingly enough, had returned to try and revive the fortunes of the British Union of Fascists. The party would undergo frequent name changes over the years, from League of Empire Loyalists to National Front. One of the most depressing aspects was the fluency that people like Daniels could command, and even a certain savage humour. Good speakers however corrupt will always win an audience and command followers, as the late Fuhrer had so abominably proved.

Overt race hatred as such was still something of a rarity in Britain at that period. Prejudice there was certainly, but the deep seated urge to kill that has since been brought to light was hardly known. So I had never had cause to analyse its causes, nor even to discuss it with my father. Sex obviously had plenty to do with it, but anti-semitism seemed a particularly puzzling phenomenon. There were few Jews in Bristol; they had odd little feast days and a funny church called a synagogue, but the few one knew at school and elsewhere had little to distinguish them from the rest of the populace. So what on earth was it that brought people like Daniels and Webster to a fever pitch of blood lust against them? Was it the fact that those one knew seemed to do rather well in their exams or build successful businesses that led to murderous jealousy from people who had failed to make the grade academically or in any other way? The puzzle remains. However the leaders of the local Labour Party were at least tuned into the dangers, and they had recently re-formed a traditional institution called the 'Watch Committee'. A group of people who kept as eye on such matters and would inform the Police authorities of any untoward developments. My father was a member, and so for a change, instead of speaking, he stood in the crowd and listened.

Towards the end of the war another crucial subject had occupied the thoughts of politically aware people like my father; how to treat the Germans when it was over. H.N. Brailsford, a left wing intellectual (though not a communist) had expressed complete confidence that once the Nazis had been removed, Germany could be trusted to welcome a return to democracy, and defend it with dedication. He wrote a book on that theme and expressed his views in papers like Reynolds News. He was vigorously opposed by one Lord Vansittart, a diplomat who expressed profound mistrust of the Germans. My father had studied the pre-war Weimar Republic closely, and strongly agreed with Brailsford. One of his heroes was a Bulgarian communist called Dimitrov. In 1934 there had been a famous trial in Leipzig, in which Dimitrov had been accused of setting fire to the Reichstag. His cool defence won worldwide admiration and he was acquitted. Pre-Nazi Germany had a reputation for justice and democracy. People like Brailsford were certain it would return, and in the intervening years they have been proved right. In the latter part of the 20th century, Germany has been involved in far fewer shooting wars than Britain.

* * *

There was a further somewhat mysterious occasion involving us which was to have considerable relevance to the future of Europe and the World.

My parents had been invited to a 'garden party' to be held somewhere South of Bristol, and they asked me to join them. I could find no reason for not going; such things occurred from time to time and, since I enjoyed driving I would be allowed to take the wheel. It was while on the way that my father muttered something to the effect that 'It would be better not to mention this to anyone'. There had never before been anything secretive about his movements and I was little puzzled but I didn't ask for reasons. I probably assumed it was something to do with the 'British Soviet Friendship Society'. This was perfectly legal still, but a climate of opinion seemed to be growing which suggested that the Russians were not entirely to be trusted. Perhaps also the Labour Party was keen not to revive memories of the famous 'Zinoviev Letter' scandal that had helped to terminate their one and only brief period of power in 1924.

In the event it was just another garden party, but I had the impression that the guests included a strong presence of Bristol University Lecturers. No surprise there. My father had been a member of the Senate ever since he achieved a higher level of medical degree, the 'Medicini Doctor' We moved around, chatted to people, ate cucumber sandwiches and cake, and admired the flower beds of this most desirable property in an area known as Cadbury Camp. It seemed quite a family occasion, with wives and small children present. Nobody made speeches, or moved votes of thanks and we all went home in the late afternoon.

It was only several years later that I began to 'construct' a hypothetical reason for the occasion. And it remains pure conjecture; recalled now to be accepted or rejected.

When the atomic bomb was made and tested at Los Alamos; the head of research, Robert Oppenheimer gathered around him all the best physicists in the allied nations. One of them in 1943 was called Klaus Fuchs, a north German protestant who had fled Hitler and studied in Britain. He had taken his Ph.D. at Bristol University, and stayed with friends who had a country house, South of Bristol. The physics department there contained a number of well known communist sympathisers, and Fuchs was a fully paid up member.

They did not however include the Head of Faculty, Sir Bernard Lovell of Jodrell Bank fame.

During all his time in USA and Britain, Fuchs passed detailed atomic bomb secrets to the Russians. When he returned from Los Alamos he was at once made head of the British Atomic Research establishment at Harwell. He had been suspected of having Russian contacts but was 'cleared' by M15 in 1945. It seems to me perfectly natural that Fuchs would want to drop in on a few old friends in Bristol. Not that a garden party would have been the occasion for any meetings with Soviet agents. Fuchs had been having those ever since 1941. His whole career reads like a Len Deighton spy thriller, with classic "drops" in Kensington Gardens, and even famous "Mornington Crescent". Arriving in USA for the Manhattan project, he made new contacts, to whom he passed sketches and information, in Central Park, Santa Fe, Boston. But he was certainly no "spy who came in from the cold ".He received the warmest of welcomes from fellow conspirators at the very top of the British Secret Service, like Philby, Burgess, Maclean and Cairncross. The whole extraordinary saga embodies a profound lesson in national stereotyping.

We have been brought up to love our macho James Bond-type heroes, rugged chaps who see off dastardly foreigners with straight lefts and technical wizardry, then bed the women sent to betray them. A whole book and film industry has grown up based on nothing other than a thumping lie, when one compares fact with fantasy. A group of devious Oxbridge intellectuals was able to hoodwink the entire Secret Sevice who employed them

Fuchs served as head of AWRE for four years. During that time he passed the most crucial information about the manufacture and detonation of the hydrogen bomb to Russian agents. In 1950 he was interviewed, and confessed. He was sentenced to 14 years imprisonment.

It seems it would have been perfectly natural for him to call in on old friends in Bristol before taking up his post at Harwell. I have nothing but the purest conjecture to offer on the matter of one little garden party. The proof is no more positive than that offered for

Neil Armstrong's landing on the moon.

And if it was he, and he was a criminal, just how serious a criminal was he? It is as well to remember that only one nation has ever used the atom bomb in anger; the U.S.A. And if the cold war became so tense, with its Berlin air lifts, its Hungaries and Czechoslovakias, its Cuban Missile Crisis, can we honestly say that the Western powers would be morally incapable of using it once again.

("Just this once, Mr. President, to stop the Russians dead in their tracks.") You have to believe the Pentagon Generals as pure as early Christian hermits not to think it possible.

And if they had wanted to do the deed, what would have stopped them but the thought of instant retaliation, on Washington, New York, San Francisco? The argument is bi-polar of course. It became known as 'Mutually Assured Destruction'. And it gave us 50 years of nail-biting 'peace'. But peace (meaning absence of world war) nevertheless.

I happen to think we may owe something to one man who just might have been at that garden party in Somerset.

Chapter 17

Like most British Cities, post war Bristol made brave efforts to build a bright new world against all the economic odds. Avery's the Wine Merchants refurbished a large building in Park Street with wood panelling and fittings from the old Mauretania, sister ship of the Lusitania. There was a grand restaurant, and at the top a circular bar called the Goldfish Bowl, with tropical fish around the walls. An impressive place for provincial kids. The Berkeley Restaurant had revived its 'The Dansants' where nice people could spin around in proper style. An ambitious Italian named Aldo Berni embarked on a plan to show the British nation that life was for living and would start to cover the map with his Steak Houses, so that 'Eating out' no longer meant fish and chips on a street corner.

The place for the young was the top floor of the Queen's Road department store, Brights. On Saturday mornings hundreds went there to see and be seen, and chat away ignoring the music trio and fashion parades. Almost as popular was a nearby ice-cream parlour called Fortes, run by a nephew of 'Mr. Piccadilly' himself; and bomb blasted Bristol even began to develop something of a New Orleans flavour when an old warehouse called "The Granary" was got ready to welcome a bowler hatted, clarinet swinging gent called Acker Bilk.

All these commendable moves took place in the face of a desperate economic situation. British overseas balances had been annihilated by the war, and our generous American cousins were now beginning to present us with bills. Worst of all was the fuel situation. Nationalisation of the mines had not brought a new flood of coal and steel. Transport was woefully inefficient and stocks of coal simply piled up in the yards, while there were frequent power cuts. Stafford Cripps with his miserly budgets became an eminence grise, targeted as a saboteur of economic recovery by the Conservatives who were determined to regain power by 1950.

As the spectre of national service grew closer, we school leavers were determined to enjoy every minute. The main fear was embodied in the words "Duration of the Present Emergency" written into Army Pay books. It might have been 2 years or even 10, depending on the men in the Kremlin and the Pentagon. My friend Austin had secured his future place in Oxford by winning a classics exhibition to Brasenose College which would entitle him to wear a long gown when he finally got there. Another classicist, Ken Binning had got into Balliol and would end up as Treasury head of Concord. In the meantime we could take temporary jobs, and I found myself reporting to the Heavy Goods yard at Temple Meads Station where gangs of seeming slaves, trundled massive loads to and fro, to the annoyance of Union leaders, who felt that students ought not to be there at all. My main achievement during that long hot summer was to upset a trolley and totally smash a gross of tomato ketchup bottles.

One hundred and forty four bottles in all; the old blues number, 'blood on the walls' perfectly describes the scene.

Once again it was friend R.P.J. Smith who came up with a way to spend such new found wealth. All he had to do was breathe the magic word "Cornwall" and we nodded in agreement. Parents had given us inspired holidays there before 1939, and now it was high time to renew acquaintance. Ray's plan was to hire a car (from a friend of his father's) and simply take off. Some camping equipment would be carried, but that was certainly not the purpose of the trip. This was a mission for sun, sea, booze and any girls who might present themselves.

The affordable transport proved to be a 1936 Ford 10, with a commendable service record. It was just about capable of taking four young males, but showed its age with distinct bearing rumble on any kind of hill. We spent the first night in Bude and succeeded in getting ourselves ejected from a British Legion dance we had gatecrashed. Efforts to pitch a tent were frustrated by Bude's notorious off-shore winds, so after a failed attempt to break into an empty caravan we slept in the car; a procedure that we followed for the next six of seven nights until aching backs hastened our return.

As we all knew St. Ives was the only place to be. We parked the car on the 'Island' and made ourselves at home. The most memorable thing about the Cornwall we saw was the total absence of 'grockles' as tourists are called. Cornwall was pure Cornwall as it had never been seen before, or would be seen again. We were known around town as the 'four mad boys from Bristol' and became almost celebrities. Our return journey was made memorable by our being passed by a large American open convertible with two highly attractive women in the front. Urged on by shouts of "get after 'em!" our driver put his foot down while we whooped encouragement. It was all too much for the ancient Ford. There was a sudden 'crack' from the front-end and the entire bonnet lifted up against the windscreen and plunged us into darkness. Running repairs just about got us home.

Nobody asked what we might have done in the unlikely event of catching up with the ladies.

This little exercise in 'laddism' did not prevent me from accompanying my parents on a more proper holiday in the Lake District. We stayed at Keswick and my father celebrated his fifty fifth birthday by climbing Skiddaw with a group of young hikers. He took his walking stick and wore a mackintosh over his suit. We were also introduced to some elementary folk dancing which stimulated an interest in ballroom dancing that my mother and father took most seriously and kept up for the rest of their lives.

'I am an Indian, my father said,' Indians love to dance'.

In the interim Joe Young had become a pioneer. He was one of the first people to think of going 'hitch-hiking' in France. He made it to the Cote d'Azur and wrote a piece about it for the local paper which included a little joke about his shoes having fallen to bits on the Promenade des Anglais.

But for most of us the time to put on ill fitting uniforms had arrived. Ray's father stumped up for a farewell dinner for his son's chums and he left to join the Hussars. Malone joined the Navy, and journeyed to Londonderry which was the only experience he had of being seaborne. Others were already abroad in 'trouble spots' like Malaya, where the last knockings of British Imperialism were still desperately in evidence as we fought the 'Communist Bandits'.

I myself had decided to opt for the R.A.F. though every scrap of enthusiasm I had once had for Spitfires and Lancasters had long since evaporated, and the whole idea now seemed like a total irrelevance. The only people that the Western powers would want to fight were Russians, and for God's sake hadn't they just about won the war for us?

But before that happened I was privileged to join in an occasion that celebrated the culmination of much of my father's political work. India was to become independent. That ex Public schoolboy Jawaharlal Nehru had made his famous speech talking about the Congress Party's "tryst with destiny", and looking towards his unforgettable "midnight hour". It was a time of widespread satisfaction among progressive Labour activists, and in England there was only one man who could be called upon to pick up the new reins of diplomatic power, my father's old colleague, Krishna Menon.

Thus we were invited to a unique celebration in London, by this Revolutionary turned High Commissioner designate. The function was to be held at India House, whence edicts on the governance of half a million Colonial subjects had been sent out since the time of Queen Victoria to mighty men like Dalhouse, Linlithgow, Curzon, and ultimately Field Marshall Wavell.

There was even a touch of irony in the trip to London itself. As we arrived to board the train I yielded to a childish impulse and went up to look at the engine. It was one of the magnificent G.W.R. King Class locomotives, standing there with its 6 foot high driving wheels, steam hissing from its valves, the driver just visible in his cab, preparing to make the mighty monster burst into ear shattering life. I walked to the front of the engine and saw that it was the pride of the fleet, the King George Vth. There on the front was a beautiful silver bell. No other British engine carried such a thing. In 1935 this very engine had been shipped to the USA for the centenary of the Baltimore and Ohio Railway. and the bell had been a 'thank you' present from the Americans It was the British Empire showing off its Railway Pioneering greatness.

The reception was a moment of true celebration, with wonderful Indian dishes; and the soft drinks flowed like wine. Krishna Menon was the centre of attention, his hands moving between 'Namaste's' and Anglo-Saxon handshakes. We stood on the edge of the throng, not seeing anyone my father knew. In any case he was quite self-effacing at this kind of gathering.

Eventually the crowd around the man of the moment thinned a little and we found ourselves fairly close. 'Aren't you going to speak to him?' I asked my father anxiously. Diffidently he moved forward to within speaking distance.

'Um, I don't know if you remember me, Mr. High Commissioner?' began my father. Menon turned and flashed a delighted smile.

'How could I ever forget you?' He answered. It was the perfect response, combining affection and long established respect. They chatted for quite some while on the current situation, with massive problems for the new Congress Government. Much of it was lost on me, but I treasure one remark of Menon's.

'Oh by the way,' he said, 'I met Churchill. He stank of alcohol...'

It was an honest comment, if well deserved and actually acknowledged by the man who had breakfasted on Champagne most of his life. A sad coda, though, on an occasion which wrote 'Finis' to an Empire that had both exceeded and outlasted its Roman model, and which in many ways had been rather more civilised.

* * *

There was one area of British power and responsibility that had indeed been acquired almost by accident, and which would now cause more pain and heart searching than any other for generations to come; Palestine.

With the dissection of the old Turkish empire after the First World War, the French and British allotted to themselves 'mandated territories'. In 1918 the French took the Lebanon, the British the area around the River Jordan that included Jerusalem and many other towns sacred to Christians, Jews and Moslems.

The Zionist movement aimed at re-establishing a Jewish 'homeland' in a small part of Palestine had begun in the thirties, and now after the Holocaust, pressure to create a separate state called 'Israel' was almost irresistible.

The United Nations were strongly in favour, the Americans were especially keen. But the British, led by Labour Foreign Secretary and one time Bristol Docks organiser, Ernest Bevin, had strong reservations. It was the British who held power there, and serving in the army was our friend Mervyn Paice, now a Sergeant in Army Intelligence.

In 1946 The King David Hotel was blown up by the Irgun, whose leader was Menachim Begin. More than a hundred people were killed, including Army personnel, Arab and Jewish civilians. The action was considered an outrage in Britain, and Army Intelligence embarked on a campaign of reprisals that involved imprisoning several thousand Zionist supporters.

Mervyn Paice and another sergeant Clifford Martin, had been maintaining close contact with Zionist sympathisers; they were in fact strongly pro Israel in their personal attitudes, but they could hardly be regarded by the Irgun as anything other then British spies. Both were betrayed and both were captured.

They were kept captive, in appalling conditions, for several days as hostages against the release of Jewish prisoners. The British authorities refused to bargain.

On July 14th, 1947 the two sergeants were taken out to an orange grove and hung. Their bodies were left hanging until found by British troops.

Naturally enough there was fury in Britain. Was this how our servicemen were to be rewarded after years of fighting for freedom and justice? The people who made the most of the dreadful happening were of course Mosley's fascists. They held protest meetings all over the country, and there were several fracas. In Bristol I was present at one such meeting. Webster embarked on an anti-Zionist tirade. He was in full flow when a message was passed up from the crowd. Webster paused and announced that Mervyn Paice's parents were in the audience and had asked him not to continue. He stood down and handed the meeting over to 'Ticky' Daniels. Sometimes British Fascists could affect good manners it seemed.

The whole context of Britain's attitude to Zionism at that time had been much debated. Certainly the key individual was Ernest Bevin, and he caused much anger in Europe and America by refusing in 1947 to allow a ship called the Exodus to land in Palestine, carrying 4,500 Holocaust survivors from France. They were sent back to live once more in squalid camps for 'displaced persons.'

There seemed absolutely no reason for the British Foreign Secretary to engage in what looked to many like anti-Semitism, and he only accepted the United Nations decision to found the State of Israel after strong pressure from the U.S.A.

The mystery also led to a revelation about the mental processes of a later Labour leader Harold Wilson himself. Intrigued by the Bevin mystery, he actually set a researcher the task of investigating Bevin's mysterious origins. It was known that he was illegitimate, his mother having been a chamber maid in a Somerset hotel. Wilson wondered if his natural father might have been Jewish; perhaps a landowner living in the area, and whether some deep rooted resentment existed. Whatever the truth about Bevin, Wilson's admission perhaps tells a little about the psychological make-up of those who became the nation's leaders.

The appalling murder of a school friend is bad enough to have to record.

Palestine was a British mandated territory, and that too must be noted in a story that deals, however marginally, with the end of Empire. But the fact that it was in Palestine adds a significance for the whole world. Palestine has had an influence out of all proportion to its size. Palestine produced the first great monotheistic religion of the world, and some would argue that Islam too should be included as a derivative. Virtually the whole of Europe, and then the Americas, created cultures in which the Old and New Testaments formed a colossal motivating source of political thought and action, for over two millenia.

In more recent times we have seen and are seeing, events in that tiny area, come to dominate the thoughts and actions of the great powers as never before. The foundation of the State of Israel was encouraged and aided by the West in an access of guilt for the horrors that one of their number had inflicted on Jews in previous decades. The fact that it involved taking a small slice of territory inhabited mainly by Muslim Arabs seemed of little consequence at the time. T.E.Lawrence and his allegiances were consigned to history. But it was not long before those Arabs built up a rising crescendo of resentment, and there is a gaping hole in the Island of Manhattan to bear witness to the fact.

In the mid-twentieth century we succeeded in creating a world in which two opposing camps, one allegedly atheistic and one allegedly Christian, confronted each other with threats of nuclear destruction. Then the wall came down and the threat from the atheist state faded away. The struggle for Iranian oil formed a link between the two kinds of confrontation, so that we now have a world, in which two camps who both claim to believe in God, confront each other with equally fearsome possibilities.

* * *

If the preceding chapters carry any message at all, it can only be to suggest that deeply buried within the human psyche are two distinct urges, which when combined lead to dire consequences for the species.

The primary urge is to bond only with those of one's fellows, who through language and traditions and dress and ceremonial, possess overwhelming kinship; and which implies rejection of those beyond the confines of nation, or race, or geography who do not possess them. The second urge is the simple refusal of our highly self aware species to believe that life itself is of any lasting consequence whatsoever in the solar scheme of things. From this comes a desperate need to believe in an 'after' life of some kind, a form of immortality which gives us a reason for existing in the first place. Without this belief we are nothing. And, when this secondary urge become structured into doctrines or dogmas, with priesthoods, and its rituals and formal means of achieving that desperately needed immortality, become locked into the primary urges of race, nation, and geographical unit, then we have a fatal mixture that leads to aggression, attack, defence, and self-sacrifice so that we respond as we have since the times of hunter gatherers.

It would seem that nothing helps the human race to declare its tribal allegiances so much as the shape of the human cranium, which lends itself to an infinite range of head coverings with which to declare allegiances; from Bowlers, Toppers, Deerstalkers, and Yarmulkas to Pickelhaubes, Stetsons, Raccoon caps, Busbies, Gandhi caps, and Turbans wound in a myriad of different ways

So while the world's real thinkers are occupied in de-constructing molecular, genetic, and astro physical realities, the world's power politicans continue to pander to the atavistic irrationality of the headgear- wearing mass of humanity, and lead us perilously in the direction of conflicts compared with which World War II was merely a little local difficulty.

Nowhere is the urge to such conflicts more brilliantly categorised than in the chapter of Jonathan Swift's unequalled satire, when it is explained to Gulliver that the Civil War in Lilliputia is being fought by two factions, the Big Endians and the Little Endians, who came to blows over the correct way to open their breakfast eggs.

And no-one has as yet improved on the advice humanity needs most to avoid its regular descent in to the vortex of savagery, than E.M. Forster, when he wrote in "A Passage to India";

"Only connect........."

Chapter 18

I had several months to while away before call up and spent much time in the company of a newly made acquaintance called Ken Sealey. He was a year my senior and had just been discharged from the Fleet Air Arm. He had actually flown Spitfires (or " Seafires" as the Navy called them), and had trained in Dallas Texas. He had undeniable style to add to his natural West Country amiability, and looked very much like the Hollywood Film star Joseph Cotten. He had been at Art School, acquired a certain sensitivity, and cut quite a dash at local hospital dances, especially when wearing his full "Mess" kit. We spent many Sundays playing tennis, or going on painting expeditions, to such an extent that my father began to worry somewhat about incipient homosexual inclinations. But he needn't have. Once when I admitted having taken out an ex girl friend of his, Ken expressed horror at the thought of shared physical experiences. In any case, my mother greatly liked him and she was a sound judge in such matters.

And then one day, the last lotus was eaten. It all had to stop. No more sitting late on park benches discussing the relative merits of Hemingway and Somerset Maugham. No more motor bike rides to paint old churches in Somerset.

My Call Up Papers arrived.

***

I would like to be able to say that I went bravely to my doom. If I did it would simply prove how close biography is to fiction. I was utterly depressed and felt it to be the end of all things lovely; home, girl friend, cars, pubs, chums.

And it was much worse than that. Padgate was the name of the R.A.F. camp in the North to which all new recruits were sent for induction. To me, snatched away from a life of total self-indulgence, it seemed to belong in one of Dante's circles of Hell. I who had been at the peak of my school career, living like a young squire, found myself in a morass of abandoned souls talking utter filth in weird accents, every second word a vile oath, and trying to eat disgusting food.

'Was this', I thought, 'the working class my father fought so hard for?'

Eventually, having been jabbed and docketed and kitted out in ill-filling apparel, I was sent to a training camp for twelve weeks to be marched about, shouted at, and told at least once daily to "get my hair cut". Evenings were spent polishing barrack room floors, burnishing coal buckets and elbow greasing boots to a mirror finish.

In fact this was all familiar stuff to most young males of my generation. The big difference was that they had left home in order to fight for freedom, and I had no idea what purpose I was supposed to be fulfilling. Or how long I might be incarcerated.

In my first twelve weeks, I achieved only one brief moment of short lived self respect. One day we were marched out to a shooting range by a smart R.A.F. Regiment Lieutenant to be shown how to load, aim and fire Lee Enfield Rifles. At last here was something I could enjoy. Confidence in my shooting skills remained as high as ever. The targets were in butts, some 100 yards away, and a man with a flag signalled 'hit' or 'miss'.

Eventually my turn came. I got down, loaded and took aim. I knew well enough it was all a matter of keeping the back sight level and controlling the breathing. I knew exactly what to do. I squeezed the trigger and cushioned the kick. To my utter horror the flag waved from side to side, signalling a miss. I took immensely careful aim and fired again. To my dismay and disbelief the flag signalled another miss. Most people would have accepted defeat. But I became possessed. Here was my one chance of self respect in all those dismal weeks, and I had failed. I was seized with a fit of arrogant self righteousness. Without pausing another second to think of the consequences, I lay down the gun, jumped to my feet, turned to the officer, saluted smartly and said in the way I had seen people do in films;

'Permission to speak, Sir.' Clearly no-one had ever behaved in this manner before. His face clouded. He said,

'Yes, what is it?'

'Sir,' I said, 'I have reason to believe that this rifle is inaccurate.'

The look on his face told me what a dreadful gaffe I had made. The Lieutenant shouted at me;

'Airman, stand at the back! Remain at attention! MOVE!'

I obeyed like lightning. As I stood there I pondered my likely fate. This was insubordination from a new recruit. I had visions of detention barracks, endless punishment drill with full back pack, being kicked and sworn at. The rest of them finished shooting.

Then the officer turned to me, face contorted with anger.

'Right, Airman,' he spat. 'This armoury is my responsibility. It is my responsibility to see that every rifle is in perfect working order. Now I am going to show you just how inaccurate this rifle is!'

The last sentence was a snarl of sarcasm. He got down and cocked the rifle. He took aim. He took very careful aim indeed. At that precise moment two prayers were rising skywards: his was that he would hit the target, mine was that he would miss.

He fired. After an excruciating second, the flag appeared. It waved slowly from side to side. The lieutenant had missed.

He jumped to his feet, without a glance in my direction. I made my face totally expressionless. There was only one way left for him to regain the ascendancy. He fell the squad in. Then he shouted, "Double March!" Our camp was nearly two miles away. By the time we arrived, we were panting and staggering with exhaustion.

For days afterwards I was the most hated man in the hut.

After three months 'square bashing' we went through our 'Passing out Parade', the ultimate spit and polish performance, men with cloths actually dusting our shining boots on the parade ground before we marched off to be inspected by an ex Regimental Sergeant Major. I could not help noticing how even the most rebellious soul like my own would eventually cave in to military discipline, and not merely obey orders like an automaton, but actually take pride in marching in unison, sloping arms to perfection, saluting correctly, the 'middle finger' just under the cap button.

Somewhere in it all there was a lesson about the essential malleability of the human species, and the misuse of power. By the end of it I felt I could have behaved like one of Hitler's S.S. men and I was profoundly grateful to escape from those who enjoyed such behaviour.

The question of what 'Trade' to adopt came next. Adolescent dreams of climbing into the cockpit of a Spitfire had long vanished; there were dozens of chaps about with 'Wings' and few aeroplanes left for them to fly. Because I had a Grammar School Education, and spoke fairly correctly it was suggested I became a Radio Operator, to which I could take no exception. Accordingly I was posted for another 12 weeks to the Radio School at Cranwell. Here I learned parrot-fashion how radios worked; antique models which still used crystals. The instructors clearly had no interest in their work and were serving out their time. But far worse than that nobody took the trouble to explain what a radio operator actually did, what happened on real airfields, what take off and landing procedures are, how many radio channels are in use, what forms of speech are used, how many log books have to be kept, what codes are used, or any of the most vital life and death routines which have to be followed in the critical matter of the take off and landing of aeroplanes.

It rapidly dawned on me that this whole great organisation that had once been geared up to a pitch of war winning efficiency, had now lost it raison d'etre and was in a state of demoralised incompetence. Nobody, to use the expression of the day, gave a monkey's toss!

The result was that when I was posted to go on duty in the Flying Control of No1, Parachute Training School, Upper Heyford, it was a sheer miracle that my own ignorance and incompetence did not result in a whole series of crashed Dakotas, and dozens of dead, rather than dead keen, members of the Parachute Brigade.

I turned up on my first day to in the Control Tower to take my seat in front of a battery of four 'headsets', loudspeakers and log books. The function of the Radio operator was in theory merely to transmit the orders of the Flying Control Officer to pilots who awaited take-off, or who were airborne and wanted to come down. In fact the operators were usually so well versed that they anticipated all the commands and gave them without having to wait for the officer's orders. Not in my case though. I hadn't a clue what 'Downwind' or Turning on Finals' or 'Runway two niner 'meant. Fortunately, the officer saw my plight.

'You new ?' he asked. I nodded glumly.

'Never done this before?' I shook my head.

'Oh God.'

He gave me a rapid course on airfield and R.T. procedures. Then he steered me through the day. He was a good guy. I started to learn what I should have been taught weeks before. But I still felt as though I had been given a week's course in Chinese and been left alone in Bei Jing.

I struggled through the next few days while Dakotas came and went, and brave men leaped out of them, desperately hoping their parachutes had been packed properly. Eventually someone must have said something to someone about me, and I was transferred to 'Night Watch.' This consisted of up to twelve hours spent alone in the control tower with all the loudspeakers turned up to maximum. If one put two chairs together, wrapped a blanket around one, it was possible to doze off with one's head resting against a loudspeaker in case an emergency call came through. It was a tedious, painful experience with 'static' dinning into one's ears all night long. I survived this for several weeks, praying that there would be no emergencies.

And then my luck ran out. Night flying was ordered. The whole place seethed with activity. The night sky was full of aeroplanes. Worst of all a different Flying Control Officer was on duty whom I had never seen before, an oldish man, said to have been ex Royal

Flying Corps. I coped as best I could. Reception on the head-sets was very poor, and sometimes it was hardly possible to hear the aircraft's identity letter - 'C, Charlie, B, Baker' or whatever. Then came a call: "Fox Able to Tower, Downwind!" which meant a 'plane was about to land. I gave him 'Clear finals.'

A few seconds later, as it seemed to me, he called 'Downwind!' again. I was puzzled. I presumed he hadn't heard me so I gave him 'Clear finals' again.

That was something I should not have done. A minute or so later there came an enormous roar of engines on full boost as a plane flew over, missing the Control Tower by inches. People around me ducked and looked in my direction. It didn't bode well.

Ten minutes or so later I heard angry footsteps outside. The door burst open and in came the Commanding Officer in full flying gear. He had chosen to-night to do "circuits and bumps" in order to keep his hand in.

'What the hell's going on?' he roared. ' There was another kite downwind ahead of me. I had to overshoot. I nearly hit the bloody tower... Show me the bloody log books!'

'I'm sorry Sir,' I stammered, 'There was so much going on that I haven't had a chance to log anything.'

'Right,' he said, then looked around, 'Where the hell's the Flying Control Officer?' Everyone looked around and began to mumble. The Officer in charge was no-where to be seen. Perhaps he had gone to the loo. I hoped he hadn't gone to dinner.

The Commanding Officer stormed out. There would be real trouble. The one person you try your hardest not to kill is your Commanding Officer. I felt sorry for the old R.F.C. man. He was bound to be Court Martialled. Almost certainly the mistake was mine. But according to Station Routine Orders, the whole responsibility was his.

I never heard what happened. Soon it appeared that RAF Upper Heyford and the Parachute Brigade could manage without my services. A fortnight later I was posted to another part of the forest, RAF Fairford.

***

I arrived at Fairford just in time for the start of the worst winter this country had experienced in living memory.

Chapter 19

The crucial factor in my early Air Force career had very little to do with aeroplanes. It had to do with my stomach, which felt permanently null and void.

RAF catering in 1947 offered a lunch of sorts at mid day, and a barely adequate 'Tea' at 5 p.m. This left up to six hours until bedtime with only a mug of water- based cocoa, and scraps of stale bread to dip into it, to help one make it through the night. I leave breakfast till last because that was where it deserved to be, since it consisted of watery porridge, and on good days, a plate of boiled cod. Yes, boiled cod.

Except, that is, for one day a month. Under the ill starred Labour government, as it plunged towards financial catastrophe, rationing of food and fuel had had to be re-introduced. Every British citizen was entitled to one egg every month, and that included the luckless folk in the Armed Forces.

At Fairford we were housed in little groups of Nissen huts, scattered as it seemed, all over the Cotswolds. So once a month, and once only, the magic words were pronounced, and repeated in hut after hut, from valley to valley, hill top to hill top.

"IT'S EGGS !!!"

Within seconds, a thousand or more men, who normally never dreamed of going to breakfast, were pulling on uniforms, struggling into gumboots, and beginning the long, desperate trek to the cookhouse, before its doors were closed at 8 a.m. On ancient bicycles, or walking or trotting, the halt and the lame, could be seen moving like men in a trance, past fields, and copses, and over hilltops from every direction, from Marston Maisey in the West to Ingelsham in the East, from Quenington in the North to Dunfield in in the South. If the names had been Chinese it would have rivalled Mao Tse Tung's Long March.

Once inside the cookhouse, the queue to the serving hatch

wound three times round the room, which was filled with the almost paradisal odour of eggs being fried in cooking fat. And just one of them was yours alone. Behind the server stood an array of the entire cook house staff, NCO's from Warrant Officer downwards, all in best uniforms, fixing every man with eyes that could have turned him to stone. For woe betide anyone who even thought of going round twice. Being shot at dawn would not have been too harsh a punishment, for any miscreant who dreamed of breaking the code of this egg starved nation. But no one did; all knew they would have been torn to pieces by their fellows, before making it to the hatch.

And if semi- starvation were not enough, early in January came the snow. It was snow such as none of us had ever dreamed possible. One woke to a blanket of snow, and by the end of the day, five more blankets had covered it. Nor was this fondly remembered warmish British snow. This was real Canadian stuff, at temperatures into double figures below zero. On the following day, shovels had been issued and we were having to dig ourselves out of our huts. I was still employed as a Radio Operator in the Flying Control Tower which I made heroic efforts to reach on a bicycle with only one pedal operational.

We were a Squadron of Halifax Bombers which had been used for towing Horsa Gliders, like those which had taken the brave men of D-Day into battle. I had managed one or two glider flights, but now the idea of "operational" was purely notional. The Halifaxes stayed in their Hangars, and snow piled up around the doors.

It was only a matter of days before the snow began to reach national disaster levels. Many R.A.F. and Army camps were closed down and people were sent on leave, since lack of road transport made real starvation a grim possibility. Our own medical officer visited the sites and took temperature readings. Up to 20 c below was registered inside some of the huts. There was almost no coal and we began to chop up tables and chairs to keep the stove alight. I managed to acquire four extra blankets. We remained unwashed and began to grow beards because the wash houses were frozen solid. The C.O. had tried to close the camp, but there was no point:

roads around Fairford had eight foot high snow drifts on them and no buses could get in or out. It was said that two Jamaican airmen had died of pneumonia.

Eventually a 'low loader', a long vehicle used for carrying aircraft fuselages, arrived and we were told to pile our beds and kitbags onto it. In groups of twenty or more we were then transported to another section where we arranged our beds, forty or so in a hut instead of twenty. They actually touched each other, but we saw the point. By now we had begun to live like Nanooks of the North.

Then one morning a Sergeant arrived carrying cans, copper tubing and welding gear. With supreme competence he fastened an oil container to the stove pipe and welded into the base a length of tube, ending in a tap. He then filled the container with engine oil brought from the hangars, and turned the tap to a slow drip. Within minutes the stove was so hot as to be almost transparent. I went outside, scooped up a mug of snow and took out my shaving brush. It had been deep inside my kitbag under my bed and was a solid lump of ice.

We felt that Sergeant deserved a D.S.O. at the very least.

In the second week of January, every available man was ordered onto the airfield to try and clear a runway. It seemed like insanity but then we were told why. The blizzard was so bad that there were villages in Staffordshire and elsewhere which had no food. The R.A.F. was going to try and fly a Halifax there with emergency supplies to be parachuted in. It was the kind of mercy mission on which the RAF based its peace time reputation.

I was on Radio duty the morning a small Auster came in to land. Pathe Newsreel had expressed the wish to cover the event and were sending two cameramen. The Flying Control officers was gazing out into the gloom waiting for it to appear. When it did one of them called out;

'My God its got skis on. He can't land on the runway. Call him' he said to me 'and tell him there's no snow,' I said I thought it had no radio. He jumped to the rack where Verey signal pistols were kept, flung open the door and fired a 'red'. Meanwhile the Senior officer who had pondered the problem intervened.

'Rubbish," he said, 'I've flown one of those things. They can land anywhere.'

He seized another Verey pistol, this time a green one, and fired. By then the plane was circling overhead. The shot went up, narrowly missing the propeller. I saw the Auster's wing tilt violently. The pilot decided that the tower was too dangerous a place to be near and came down in the snow some distance off.

By the following day the whole operation was on in deadly earnest. The Control Room was packed with people. The Halifax, crammed full of provisions, was on the runway, warming up its engines. There was a buzz of conversation among officers. I heard someone ask who was flying it.

'McIntyre,' said someone.

'He knows what he's about,' said another.

It was well known that Squadron Leader McIntyre had a D.F.C. and was something of a war hero. There was much muttering about the weather and shaking of heads. The conditions were judged to be abominable and only extreme emergency would justify such a flight. All the runway lights were lit and there were two fire tenders and 'blood wagons' standing by. On board the Halifax was a full crew and the two newsreel cameramen. The pilot indicated his readiness. He was given 'Clear take off'. The roar of the massive bomber was a familiar enough sound, but this time it seemed to have a specially dramatic quality about it. Everyone crowded to the windows and we saw the plane almost lumbering along the runway, taking an unduly long time to get airborne, and then almost at once disappearing into the murk.

One might have expected someone to wish the pilot 'good luck', but such expressions were never used among aircrew. There seemed to be a kind of pretence, in contradiction to all experience, that nothing could go wrong, and all would return safely. Men who had lost friend after friend in action still seemed to cling to the illusion. Without it they would have had to quit the service.

I went off duty feeling that for once I had taken part in an operation of real value.

It was only when I arrived at work next morning that I learned the truth.

The Halifax had crashed in thick fog on Grindon Moor in Staffordshire. All on board had been killed.

Few comments were heard, and certainly no complaints. To the older wartime hands, this was simply the name of the game. To me as a raw recruit who had once been starry eyed about the Air Force, it was a short sharp reminder that the people who had actually lived with the likelihood of violent death day after day, were really rather special; and I had absolutely no evidence whatsoever that I had any of the qualities necessary to become one of them. Perhaps, secretly, I counted myself lucky.

Soon after the event I decided to to try and make a break for freedom. I had bought an old and unreliable motorbike while at Cranwell, and it offered the only hope. I went to the HQ building and applied for leave.

'Where on earth d' you think you might be going?' Asked an incredulous Corporal in the Adjutant's Office.

'Home' I said.

'And how d' you think you'll get there?'

'By motorbike.' I said. 'Best of Bloody British luck', came the inevitable comment.

My motorbike was a dreadfully ancient Norton, and had broken down so often I had almost abandoned it. But these were desperate times. To cover the ninety miles or so to Bristol was a problem for compasses rather than maps. Roads were scarcely discernible and only occasionally did the top of a sign post appear above the snow. I felt like Evans, rather than Scott of the Antarctic. I had nicknamed the motorbike Boanerges, (since I fancied myself as 'Aircraftsman Shaw'). It spluttered into life after much heating of plugs, and I found that if I kept both legs stiffly out in front of me, my feet would act as outriggers in the snow.

The journey was more wrestling than riding, but after an exhausting couple of hours sliding and skidding and swearing, I made it to Cirencester without having to ditch in the snow more than a couple of times. This was half way home, but I feared I might not make it, so I abandoned the bike in someone's back yard, leaving a note which said, 'Will collect when it thaws.'

I made my way to the railway station and was told, that a train would be running, but "only to Didcot." This was in completely the wrong direction, but in those days one emulated the American hobo and took any train, anytime, in any direction.

Eventually, at Didcot, I found a packed train which was lurching more in hope than schedule to Bristol Temple Meads. It took me six shivering hours to complete the eighty mile journey.

Leave under such conditions was mostly a matter of getting cleaned up and eating some proper food. But there was a warm family welcome, I made it to the Old Tavern with my brother and I also made contact with my old friend Austin.

He had joined the R.A.F. at the same time, but always managed to get himself posted to places a short easy distance from home. He had begun the pattern of life which would eventually see him on the boards of the nation's most powerful financial establishments. On this occasion he had joined the station band, became music arranger, and came home every weekend on the pretext of purchasing music manuscripts. It was what was called in the Air Force 'working a flanker.' You could get away with almost anything if your excuse was improbable enough. However, even Austin did not totally escape the 'big freeze'. Seated in the pub, he told me, with an expression of utter revulsion how he had been put in charge of a party and told to clear out the toilets in the womens' quarters nearby, which were totally iced up.

'It was the most disgusting job any one has ever been given since time began.' he said, between tight lips.'Utterly, unspeakably disgusting. I had to use a hammer and chisel on every bog. It was utterly unspeakable.'

I stayed at home for as many days as I dared, and on my return to Fairford I made a life-changing decision. If I was going to suffer this kind of existence for goodness knew how many years, the least I could do was try and get some foreign travel out of it. I might be sent to India, which I knew I must visit some day. So I marched to the office again and requested a posting to the Far East. It simply did not occur to me to me that thanks to the Labour Party and my father, no more British troops would ever again be sent to defend the British Empire in India.

However I did not have long to wait. One could always rely on the Air Force to do the right thing by its men. My posting to the mystic East came through within weeks. It was to Watton in East Anglia.

Chapter 20

Per Ardua ad Australia

Thus far my Air Force career had begun to implant in me, if
not a future "fear of flying", a decided nervousness about what went
on in Control Towers during an aircraft's all important take off and
landing procedures. Nevertheless the authorities still felt it worth
while to send me on a course at Watton to learn about a new use for
Radar called 'Ground Controlled Approach.' If they had decided to

replace my dubious skills with some new technology, that was fine by me. However nothing much happened for a couple of weeks until one day a corporal stopped me in the road. He confirmed that I was Aircraftsman Datta, and said with serious expression;

'Well, a posting's come through for you. It's to Japan.' I must have looked at him in disbelief.'Well,' he went on, 'It's lying on my desk right now. I can lose it or process it. It's up to you. You want to go to Japan?'

'Oh yes please,' I said, 'Thank you very much Corp. I'd really like to go to Japan. Thank you very much. Very decent of you Corp.'

I was posted to a dispersal camp called in Lancashire called Burtonwood, and joined a motley collection who were going to Egypt, The Yemen, Singapore, Hong Kong and Japan, everywhere of course, except India. It was going to be one hell of a trip; I would see half of the world on the way. I had never felt such excitement. After a week or so I drew some extraordinary kit which included tropical gear, and thick, thigh length woollen socks, and an Australian type khaki hat. Clearly no-one had a clue what the weather might be like. Briefly I befriended a highly intelligent Sergeant called Bernard Lewis who was a composer, and had signed on in order to provide an estranged wife with an income, while he continued writing string quartets. He was nicknamed 'Birdbrain' and he greeted hutmates returning from a night's drinking with raucous shouts of "Did you get it in?"

We had a few drinks together, and he condemned Stalin and spoke strongly in favour of Trotsky, We both agreed Salvador Dali was brilliant.

It was about a week later that a Sergeant spoke to me outside the hut. He asked me my name and when I told him, he said.

'This is nothing personal you understand, but what nationality are you?'.

'British,'I said. He pondered a moment and then said; 'Well, what about your father, where was he born?'

'Ah, India,' I said, beginning to suspect some unpleasantness.

'Well, I'm very sorry,' he said, 'but there's a problem. There's been an order through that no coloured troops are to be sent to Japan.'

If he had picked up a fire bucket and hit me with it, I would not have been more stunned. His words seemed utterly senseless. He repeated the 'nothing personal' bit. My mind raced ahead. The truth about my origins only rarely came into my conscious mind. There was little need for it to do so. If it did I usually found a way to take evasive action But this was different It was going to put my whole plan into jeopardy. To be told my trip was off, and for some utterly imbecile and disgraceful reason, put me on my mettle as never before. I thought hard. I recalled having been told in the early days about a process called 'Redress of grievance'. To save my sanity this is what I had to try and do whatever it took.

'Request permission to see the Commanding Officer,' I said as calmly as I could. The Sergeant knew the rules of the game.

'Right,' he said. 'Report to the Adjutant's office at 2 p.m.'

My interview, with some sort of Senior Officer was brief, formal, and for me exceedingly risky. I knew that all I could do was make a desperate attempt to play politics; and if it came unstuck I could be in the deepest water possible. I was marched in, removed my cap, stood to attention and explained to a somewhat perplexed Flight Lieutenant about being taken off the draft and for what reason, and asked for the decision to be reversed.

He pondered for a moment and then said;

'Can't be done airman,' he said. 'If it's a rule, it's a rule and that's that.'

I requested permission to speak, took a deep breath and said,

'Beg your pardon sir, but if I am taken off the draft, for such a reason I shall have to take the matter up with my M.P, he is Sir Stafford Cripps, and he is the Air Minister.'

I could hear the words echoing inside my head as I said them. I was taking an awful chance. Wisely I didn't add that he was a friend of my father. I didn't have to. The officer glared at me, realising that I was someone a bit different, and here was a situation that if it got out of hand, could easily upset his easy life while he was waiting for demob.

I meanwhile was fighting to keep calm. What I had done was break ranks. To try and go outside the omnipotent hierarchy of the services was the ultimate crime. If they called my bluff the charge would virtually amount to mutiny.

The officer picked up his phone. I heard him pass over all the details to his senior officer who asked the classic racialist question, to which his reply was.

'He looks like a typical Indian to me.' There was further muttering. I was told to dismiss and wait outside. I had to wait all of ten minutes. Then the Sergeant came out.

'Well,' he said, 'You've done it. You can stay on the draft to Japan. But watch your step, son.'

'Thank you Sarge,' I said.

I had the rest of the day to come to terms with the situation. The first worry was purely practical. Stafford Cripps was in fact M.P. for an adjacent constituency; and he was no longer Air Minister. A good prosecuting lawyer could have made mincemeat of me if the officers had turned nasty. In fact there had been more than one R.A.F. mutiny and the ringleaders had been given long sentences But the war was long over, and perhaps even the military establishment was nervous about the new found power of the Labour Party.

The rest of my angst was purely personal. I could count on the fingers of one hand the number of situations of race prejudice I had been involved in. The rugby coach had been a bit unpleasant on one occasion. There was the business of June's father. But by and large I had been let off lightly I supposed.

It was the author of the imperishable "Catch 22" who wrote somewhere else that "If you ever manage to forget you're a Jew some Goy is sure to remind you". I grew up in a world, not, as it seemed then, greatly obsessed with racialism. The facts of one's parenthood occupied a repressed stratum of one's consciousness. It was ever present, but not dominant. Not nearly as serious as being born with a cast in ones eye, or having a stammer. Certainly no way as disturbing as being an orphan or having a serious limp. But then on occasion, some one, or some thing reminded one of one's idiosyncrasy. Something like a too honest remark by a child, or a "joke" from a teacher who should have known better, or even a well meant enquiry about one's origins, or as in the present case, an enquiry from an overly officious sergeant. Racialism as a social curse in Britain did not reach its zenith until a certain de-tribalised Welsh quasi- intellectual called Powell, used it to further his political career after large numbers of immigrants arrived from the fast fading Empire that he himself had been dispossessed of. So some might argue, we brought it on ourselves; others would say we merely gave the British an opportunity to widen their horizons, and learn to behave in a civilised fashion.

By a remarkable irony, it was my father's old friend and my namesake David Garnett, who in his visionary manner, foresaw the way matters might develop. His novel "The Sailor's Return" portrays a Briton returning from overseas with an African wife. He takes over a pub in Surrey, and slowly but inexorably a wall of resentment builds up among the locals. Published in 1925 it tackles the subject head on, in a way that even Joseph Conrad failed to do.

In my pre-embarkation situation the upset was not in fact something I took personally, but it had wide social implications. It was the simple idea of 'no coloured troops to Japan' that incensed me. What coloured troops were they talking about for God's sake? There were only a handful of Jamaicans in England. And as far as Indians were concerned, the Indian Army had been in the thick of the fighting from Eritrea to Monte Cassino, with Gurkhas and Sikhs winning more V.C.'s than the British themselves.

It seemed like a ruling of total lunacy, a hangover from the days of Empire still persisting in the military clubs of the West End. Had none of them heard of what Gandhi and Nehru and people like my father and Krishan Menon had done to their precious Empire? It was all over chums, go away and write your memoirs.

And in its last days most of it had become a performance of utter fatuity, clung to by a Royal Family who depended for their continuance on the dunderheads who gave their ill-educated offspring paper Union Jacks to wave, whenever some idiot drove by, propped up by some uniformed skinhead.

When the Queen Mother died they gave her a twenty one gun salute. What on earth did the old girl need twenty one big bangs for? Did St. Peter have to be warned to move smartly to open the pearly gates because a member of the British Royal Family was on her way in? And if she'd been a nice old thing as they often are, why Field Guns? Field Guns were for blowing people to bits, for killing Highlanders at Culloden, or the fathers of French or German children, or the fellows in Italy who died on my brother's open air operating table.

Even if the Empire has long gone, its militaristic trappings have to be kept alive to keep a disfunctional Royal Family, direct descendants of history's most consistent serial killers, in a preposterous fantasy of power and popular loyalty.

Was it their hangers on who didn't want any coloured troops in Japan?

***

Chapter 21

When we arrived at Southampton docks and I saw the ship waiting to take me half way round the globe, I was prepared to forgive the Air Force and the British Empire everything. She was a beautiful single funnel liner, close on 20,000 tons, painted white with a blue line running round her. Her name was Dilwara, after a famous Indian Temple, and that gave a clue to her origins. She was owned by the British India Steamship Navigation Co., one of the world's biggest merchant fleets; part of the lifeline, via the Suez canal, that had kept the Empire at the peak of its power for a hundred years or more.

I responded well to the call of the seas, which could not be denied. As we rolled through the bay of Biscay, I soon acquired sea legs and never felt a trace of sickness. The ship was packed with troops. I didn't take to the tangled web of the hammock, and learned to sleep on the bare deck, beneath the stars. Excitement soon dispelled any aches and pains. When we were well under way, there came a quite unexpected reminder of our Imperial heritage. From the bowels of the ship, there appeared a team of twenty or so Indian seamen, Bengalis known as Lascars, who went down on their knees with buckets and brushes, and advanced in a single line along the deck, furiously scrubbing every inch of it. It was clearly no job for a white man. But it showed a proper concern for shipboard hygiene, and had been done this way ever since the days of Captain Bligh. So I swallowed my anti-Imperialist instincts.

As we passed Gibraltar, however, I was also reminded, with total justification, that I too was one of the lower forms of animal life in His Majesty's Air Force. Six of us were called out and told to report to the Galley for potato peeling duties. The quantity of such a staple to be consumed by a thousand troops can be imagined. We sat around a vast tub, which was regularly replenished from a wall of sacks. Peelings were heaved out down a perilous looking chute, straight into the foaming seas below. We spent at least five hours at the stint every day. Soon hands were as hard as iron. At times I longed to be back in the Sixth form. A bond of suffering was formed between us, which lasted all the way to Japan. The others were a preponderance of Liverpudlians, like Mac, Stan and Barney, but above all there was 'Butch' Curwen. He was the strongest man I would ever meet. 'Lenny' had nothing on him. He was about 6 feet tall, and slightly overweight, but he could put headlocks on any two of us simultaneously, which came close to breaking necks. All in pure fun of course.

Our first stop was Port Said in Egypt, and it exploded into eyeballs with sights and sounds that had hitherto existed only in travel books. The men in the 'bum' boats, clamoured to sell leatherware, decorated with camels and palm trees, and brassware, and one man even held a book aloft. When one decoded his English, ("Ladychattlyslubbah") one realised that it was D.H. Lawrence's most infamous novel, still at that time banned in England. The journey through the Suez canal must have been familiar to hundreds of thousands of British servicemen and civilian servants of the Empire. Perhaps to many of them it was just a trip on a boat in a very hot climate ('Port out, Starboard home'). I found it a colossal stimulus to the imagination. The sight of seemingly endless desert sands sweeping away on either side triggered off romantic responses I had no idea I possessed. I felt something of what must have motivated great adventurers like Burton, Doughty, Lawrence and Freya Stark who felt impelled to take on and conquer those fearful, burning, life and death wastes.

Merely to think about them brings on a sense of humility, since they were not just explorers, they knew Euripides and Herodotus, and had substantial academic achievements behind them which made one's school learning seem utterly puny. As the Sinai desert, and the Hejaz, and the whole length of Saudi and the Yemen slid by I could hardly consider myself any kind of pioneer, since all I had to do was sit on the deck of a fine ship, turning a very deep brown in the sun, and drinking frequent mugs of tea. And the only price to be paid was peeling potatoes, which, I had to admit, in comparison with those great names, was just about my mark. Nor did I, nor any of my mates, nor indeed any of the world's leaders, have the slightest inkling that within ten years this was to be the setting for the last gasp of the British Empire, brought on by Anthony Eden's desperate attack on Egypt to snatch the Suez canal back from Nasser. And leading to unending conflicts that would bring the world close to a series of vicious wars about God and oil.

After a week or so at sea, the desirability of some form of entertainment became the prime concern of those in charge of us. So far the main amusement seemed to be the sight of the Officers' wives wearing very short shorts, playing deck quoits on the deck above ours. Hundreds of testosterone charged men crowded the stern of the ship to admire their sporting skills, a pretence which fooled no one.

There was an amateur talent contest, loudly applauded for the bravery of the participants rather than any talent; and an army 'squaddy' whom I recognised as Beavis from Bristol Grammar School, tried to organise giant rugby scrums with hundreds of men pushing against each other. This had to be abandoned because the losers were in danger of going overboard.

Then, inevitably, came the boxing match. For some reason we spud bashers were considered good candidates, but only in one case was it justified. I was pushed into opposing Stan Hume, and was overcome with relief when he backed out. I really do not have a nose for boxing. Another chum called 'Barney', an ex Blacksmith, was compelled to enter the lists, and of course the mighty 'Butch' Curwen was bound to top the heavyweight bill. What actually happened ended for all time any schoolboy notions I had of what boxing was about. Barney was tough enough, but he found himself up against an R.N. stoker who had clearly had some professional experience. The sailor pursued him around the ring with clinically accurate straight lefts. Barney survived the three rounds but only just. The day's real horror story came from the fists of everybody's dear friend 'Butch'. A man called Sergeant Hodge, a large Rugby Forward, upheld the honour of the Sergeant's Mess by going in against him. Before three rounds were up, 'Butch' had reduced him to a shambling, bloodied hulk, in need of urgent medical attention.

Later, in Japan Butch became a legend. I realised that one of the reasons there were so many boxers, weight lifters, and rugby players on our draft was that the Australians rather enjoyed beating up the occasional 'Pommy'. When Butch Curwen arrived everything became miraculously peaceful; not a single Aussie lifted a finger from that moment on.

None of this, however, could diminish my pleasure in the rest of the voyage. We reached Ceylon and had a few days to enjoy beautiful vistas, temples and snake charmers. At sea I photographed Dolphins sporting in the bow waves. It was a moment of pure magic when an exquisitely shimmering, blue and silver flying fish came through a porthole and landed on the table. This was the road to Mandalay after all. By then my potato stint was over, and when we reached Singapore I could enjoy all the sights and sounds that so captivated writers like Maugham and Conrad.

This was the Singapore of old, with its sampans and cheongsams, its Raffles hotel and its street vendors with glowing braziers, offering sambals and satays and a host of unknown delights. It was also the impregnable British fortress, bristling with guns pointing out to sea, that the Japanese had simply come in and conquered on bicycles. By now the new cold war was already under way in Malaya, but a tough Chinese politician called Lee Kwan Yu was planning to sweep away the last vestiges of Empire and turn his city into a skyscraping showpiece of global capitalism.

As usual we British servicemen had not an inkling of what was really going on. There are few so uninformed as the uniformed.

The Indian ocean gave way to the South China Sea, and we turned Northwards into colder latitudes. It was as we made for Hong Kong that the thus far amiable ocean decided to show us what it was really capable of. We caught the edge of a Typhoon, which sank many fleeing fishing boats and lasted for three days. At its height the Dilwara rocked about alarmingly, swaying sideways, so that the anchor clanged scarily against the ship's side. We all grew somewhat thoughtful; I tried to reassure myself by gazing around at the massive iron bulkheads, with their huge rivets, feeling sure that such strength, forged in the shipyards of the Clyde, could withstand the worst that nature could do. I was just about preparing to try and get some sleep, when I was surprised to see a man I knew well, groping along a passageway towards one of the ladders. His name was Dave Cooper and he was a Sergeant Air Gunner who had survived a full tour of duty in Lancaster bombers over Germany. He was carrying a roll of bedding and his face looked ashen.

'Where you going, Dave?' I asked. 'Up on deck,' he snapped back. 'I'm not stopping down here. It's too bloody dangerous.' I could scarcely hide my astonishment.

'Surely of all people you're not scared?' I asked. 'Not staying down here,' he repeated, 'I'm getting up on deck.' I certainly had no wish to mock but I couldn't resist asking,

'But Dave, how many Ops did you do in Lancasters?'

'Twenty bloody six.'

'Twenty six! You're just about the bravest man on the boat. Surely this bit of a storm doesn't worry you ?'

'I don't give a damn what you say,' he replied, heading for a nearby ladder.

He left me puzzled. Could a man who had spent night after night in a flimsy aeroplane, with shells bursting all round his head, really be that scared at sea?

Dave Cooper was no coward, just a man out of his element, it seemed. Or perhaps his nerves were already shot to pieces.

Later we learned that the Typhoon had been bad enough to damage a Royal Navy Cruiser. Perhaps I had simply been showing blissful ignorance.

Six long life enhancing weeks after we had left Southampton the Dilwara crossed the Inland Sea of Japan, and anchored at a port in Honshu called Kure. As we docked we crowded the rail eagerly to take in the sights of this strange, but formidable country we had come to occupy. I did not have to wait long for a verbal reaction. I was standing next to Mac, the weightlifter, and he was staring down at a gang of stevedores, unloading cargo and being barked at by the man in charge. Mac was fixing him with a glare and almost snorting.

'Look at that bastard down there,' he said, 'Look at that bastard,' The object of his suppressed rage was a little man wearing Japanese army fatigues. He wore thick glasses, and an army cap and displayed prominent teeth when he shouted. He looked as if he had stepped straight out of the famous American war-time poster with the caption - 'Know Your Enemy.' Mac rose to his theme.

'My brother was imprisoned in Changi,' he shouted, 'then they made him work on the railway. They gave him a terrible time. He got Beri Beri. When he came home he was swollen up like a barrage balloon. He damned near died. I tell you Dave, if one of those bastards steps out of line with me, I'll kill him with my own hands.'

We were assembled and marched to board a waiting troop train. I was quite glad to get away from Mac. As the train moved slowly through the countryside, past paddy fields, and over innumerable bridges, I began to relish the countryside. It was utterly and undeniably beautiful, with mountains and rivers on all sides.

After an hour or so the train slowed and stopped at a station. I heard a female announcer calling a name. It sounded something like "Roshma, Roshma" but meant nothing to me. Then came a moment of great hilarity in my compartment. On the other side another train had pulled in, and there, perfectly framed by the window, sat a Japanese woman, breast-feeding a baby. The effect on eight sexually repressed British youths came close to ecstasy. They rocked too and fro, in an access of laughter and lust. The Japanese mother looking across, caught their inane grins and at once began smiling and bowing as she continued giving breast to the child. The result in our compartment was near hysteria.

One could only imagine that she was responding with gratitude to the respectful admiration at her maternal performance from these unknown occupiers of her country! What nice, sensitive, respectful people these young British men must have been, so to admire her moment of triumphant motherhood. A forest of joyful grins on all sides, feelings of warm humanity that transcended all national barriers.

As the train began to move again, my colleagues relaxed with their cherished memory. I glanced out of the window on my side to take in a view of the city we were leaving. Again I heard the girl's voice, "Roshma"........

I found myself staring in amazement at the scene to my left. There were roads, but no buildings. A criss-cross layout of streets, but nothing lining them. A map with no pictures. And almost no people. No houses, no shops, no vehicles, no movement. Here and there piles of disordered bricks and concrete slabs, and twisted iron girders pointing crazily at the sky.

I heard the station announcer's voice one last time, growing distant now. It had a dying fall to it. Then, suddenly I knew what she was saying.

It was "Hiroshima". Pronounced properly, more like 'Roshma', with that sad, sad note, as though she was commemorating some recent act of infamy, perpetrated on her very own family, friends and neighbours.

I called to the others to take a look.

'We've just passed through Hiroshima,' I said. One or two understood as I had. But for the benefit of the rest, I felt obliged to offer an explanation.

'It's where we dropped the atom bomb', I said.

Chapter 22

The traditional landscape of Japan seemed to have been crafted deliberately to overwhelm the senses with beauty. Swirling streams flow down from volcanic, pine clad hills, under little wooden bridges, past an embroidery of paddy fields towards seas dotted with rocky islands. The captivated observer can point a camera in any direction and produce a photographic gem; nature has worked out the composition already. And beautiful as it is, it is already familiar from the wood cuts and ceramics that have delighted European artists for many generations. Delicate wooden houses with up-tilted ridge lines, the temple Torii with their perfect symmetry, women in their floral obis are all as they were drawn by geniuses like Hokusai and Hiroshige. How privileged indeed we were to see the land in its time honoured state before greedy monsters like Nissan and Mitsubishi could begin to swallow it in huge mouthfuls.

The name of our R.A.F. Base was Iwakuni. It had been the main training camp for Japanese navy pilots, and was lavishly appointed, with spacious huts, a large dining hall, a comfortable cinema, a well equipped gymnasium, an indoor swimming pool and a number of indoor heated plunge baths, an indulgence adored by the Japanese. Apparently it was from this aerodrome that many of the Kamikaze pilots had flown; they were clearly given every luxury before going to die for their Emperor. For us too the catering was of the highest standards the Australians could provide. After past experience it took me some time to adjust to a diet of lamb chops, steaks and saute potatoes, with a breakfast of any number of eggs one wanted, and a choice of marmalades including one called 'passion fruit'. Naively I had to enquire whether this was a joke, or did such fruit really exist.

The Aussies and Kiwis must have considered us cave dwellers.

Each hut had a Japanese youth to clean and tidy, and I was told nothing needed to be locked away. Honesty was a Japanese religion. I was sent to work in the 'Homer', a direction finding van on the edge of the airfield which gave bearings to any pilots needing a 'fix'. It was crewed by three men who had been together in India. They hardly welcomed my arrival but in all charity I think this was merely the typical response of old chums who had been together a long time and didn't need a new face. In any case I only had the vaguest notion how to carry out the necessary direction finding procedures. They let me drink tea with them, but that was the limit of their hospitality. Maybe it was just as well.

My spud-bashing chums and I settled in well together and soon learned that one of the main activities on the base was the 'black market' Iwakuni was a small country town, but a number of shops, and a brothel, had sprung up for the occupation. We could spend our pay in a camp shop buying soap, cocoa, chocolate, Horlicks and Bournvita, and sell them to the friendly sons of a nearby farmer, or other traders. Most of our yen were spent on cameras, personal jewellery like "Damascene"rings, and ceramics; a local shop was packed every day with Australian officers' wives buying much prized old Satsuma. It was hardly a black market in the 'Third Man' Style; the Japanese were very short of food, and we felt we were supplying a need. I took the opportunity of buying an excellent pair of silver framed spectacles at the local opticians. Making conversation with the owner it occurred to me to ask if he had been able to hear the atomic bomb explosion from not too distant Hiroshima.

'But of course' he said, with something of a smile at my naivety in asking. Occasionally one heard of someone patronising the local brothel, but by and large we were not too depraved, and sport raised its ugly head more often than sex.

We made occasional use of the gymnasium and in one moment of bravado Stan and I decided to swim in the open air pool. It was late November and a sprinkling of snow had already fallen. Watching Australians gave vent to oaths of astonishment at two loony Brits plunging in, and swimming a couple of lengths. Needless to say we did not tarry at the poolside. I also played one game of Rugby which as it transpired would be my last. On the way to the ground I saw that all participants had their knees well wrapped in bandages.

When I enquired why, I was told cryptically "You'll see."

The pitch had been laid out on an acre of sand, totally grass free, but liberally sprinkled with pebbles. It was hard to say which of my two sporting indulgences had been the most painful

We got on well with the few Japanese we met. One morning I was walking past the Motor Transport depot, carrying my camera. Friend 'Mac' appeared at the door, followed by two young Japanese He hailed me;

'Over hear Dave! Come on! You've got to take a picture. Me and these two lads here. Bloody marvellous they are. Lovely lads. Never seen such workers. Come on!'

With that he wrapped his arms around the shoulders of his two assistants. I clicked, clicked again.

'Bloody lovely boys they are,' Mac. re-iterated 'I'm going to send a photo to my brother.' This of course was the brother who had been a Japanese P.O.W.

The camp cinema gave us a regular diet of American wartime 'B' movies which were greeted with much derision. Errol Flynn was shown winning the war in Burma, and a new star arrived pretending to pilot Flying Fortresses. He had a charming smile, a nice hair do, and his name was Ronald Reagan. An interesting feature of the shows was that 'Butch' Curwen was always last to arrive. He picked up a chair from the back and carried it to the front, where he sat on it after looking around and daring anyone to object. No-one did. I also noticed that in the street, officers also tended to salute him first, and said, 'Hello Butch.' He had served several years in the Army before joining the R.A.F. and one night we worked out that he had spent more time in Detention barracks that I had spent in the R.A.F.

Idly scanning a notice board one day an announcement caught my attention. It referred to the forthcoming marriage of H.R.H. Princess Elizabeth to her Greek fiancee who was called 'Philip' To commemorate this occasion of national rejoicing the R.A.F. proposed to mount a special parade in the Emperor's Palace in

Tokyo. Volunteers were requested to sign below. It looked to me like a unique opportunity to see Tokyo, with several days at leisure there, so I appended my signature. The price, a bit of drilling, was not too high, I felt; I had no antipathy towards Greeks, and it was better than peeling potatoes. In due course we were assembled to be kitted out with new uniforms, parade ground webbing, rifles and bayonets; the proper fourteen inches of cold steel that was supposed to frighten the German machine gunners on the Somme. I noted that I seemed to be the only British volunteer. The others were all Aussies and New Zealanders. Patriotism had its limits after all, and perhaps the rest of the Brits had been taught by their fathers never to volunteer for anything.

For a week or so we paraded and drilled and reached a standard that we felt qualified us for the Horse Guards. Our contingent of over fifty travelled to Tokyo on a special train which took a day and a night. Its slow pace allowed us to enjoy the unparalleled beauty of a railway line that skirted the Inland Sea, passed famous sights like the sunken temple of Miyajima, castles like Himeji, and beautiful parks with ancient pagodas at Nara and Kyoto.

At 4a.m. on the second day I got up to use the lavatory and looked out from the end of the corridor. The sight took my breath away. There, seeming to hang in the sky, was the snow capped peak of a vast and totally symmetrical volcano, many thousands of feet high. I went back and called a New Zealander to come and take a look.

'It has to be Fujiyama,' I said. Others joined us in silent wonder at the incredible mountain. It was impossible not to feel something of the reverence that possessed the soul of every Japanese. Even young, no-nonsense Westerners felt a momentary touch of something akin to spirituality.

By the middle of that day we ceased being tourists, and became soldiers again. As if to labour the point, there came an incident for which I can find no explanation, and which could have had unpleasant consequences. As we climbed from the train with rifles and packs, the Aussie Drill Sergeant in charge made us form up in column of three marching order. He barked the orders "shoulder arms," then "order arms"; perhaps, we thought, to wake us up and get us into some sort of parade ground readiness. No surprises there, but next, to everyone's surprise be gave the order "Fix bayonets!" We did so, smartly enough. Then he gave the order,

"Right turn!"

Before we knew what he intended, he shouted,

"Rifles at the trail! Follow me! Double March!"

He then ran to the head of the column and led the way down some steps, into a tunnel which led to the Tokyo Underground.

It was a busy time of day and the tunnel was full of Japanese commuters. In a state of total shock at the unimaginable sight of fifty men, charging and flashing cold steel at them, they flung themselves sideways to escape. It seemed to me a manouevre of total madness. Not least was the unpleasantness of each of us having a man clattering along behind him carrying a lethal weapon, the point inches behind his rear quarters. Those at the front ran faster and those at the back ran faster still to catch up. If it was pure nastiness for us it was a nightmare for the Japanese commuters as we rounded each bend in the tunnel, seemingly intent on bayoneting the first man or woman we saw. Mercifully the tunnel was not long and by some miracle no-one was killed or wounded. The Sergeant halted us. We replaced our bayonets, then stood at ease, waiting to board a waiting bus as though it was all in a day's work.

To this day I have no explanation for it. Many Australians had suffered badly at the hands of the Japanese. Perhaps our man had a brother, like Mac, and this was one small way of gaining a moment's revenge. Perhaps he really would have liked to kill a Japanese. Ours not to reason why.

After our bayonet charge, the parade itself was something of an anti-climax. Our webbing was rendered all white by a typically Australian trick of dipping it all in buckets of cellulose paint. We were taken to an area just outside the Emperor's Palace. We formed up and marched about as trained. We had rehearsed a movement known as a "Feu de Joie", in which the rifle is hoisted onto the shoulder and a fusillade is fired. Unfortunately the necessary blank cartridges failed to turn up, so that was cancelled. Nor was there any kind of band to march to. Nor did I see the Emperor peering nervously out from one of his windows. Nor did any of the Japanese passers by take any notice of us. Should I ever meet the Duke of Edinburgh I shall be happy to tell him that what we did on that day was entirely worthy of him.

We enjoyed our well earned sojourn of rest and sightseeing in Tokyo for which I concentrated on art galleries and temples. There were one or two further incidents of what might be termed colonial machismo. One evening I was waiting for the last train out to our billets. When it arrived the guard indicated that the reserved carriage was full up, and moved to close the door. There were three very tough looking Australian Army Sergeants standing next to me. One of them immediately removed the guard's hand from the button; the other two stepped inside and invited all the occupants to leave the carriage, or face consequences. They were all American G.I.'s, all young and all had Japanese girl-friends; Americans were allowed to fraternise but we were not. To my amazement they all obliged without a word of protest. The three sergeants and I went home in an empty carriage.

On another occasions, it was I who was in danger from the Australians. I had joined a couple of New Zealanders who proposed to visit something called the "Union Jack" club, which had presumably been founded to enable different members of the Commonwealth services to get to know each other better. We reached it by rickshaw, a form of transport that modern Japanese find it hard to credit ever existed in Tokyo. I overcame a brief moment of bad conscience at being hauled along by an oldish looking man, who nevertheless seemed wiry and fit. Since the British authorities in their unwisdom had banned Japanese female company, there was little to do but drink strong beer and listen to the music of a quartet playing light music. A strong contingent of Maoris was present, and an interesting moment arrived when they struck up "Now is the Hour". This had been adopted by all Maoris as their 'national' anthem, and to a man they rose and walked to the dais, proceeding to eyeball the Japanese musicians as if daring them to play one wrong note. The Japanese proceeded to perform with unflinching impassivity, and gave a perfect rendering. The Maoris returned to their seats, honour satisfied.

I spent most of the evening chatting to my friends, mostly about Rugby and the war, which one of them had spent in England. We were interrupted by the arrival of three men in Australian army uniforms,making towards the exit. They were seemingly very drunk and propping each other up. They stopped at our table and the middle one suddenly addressed me.

'Hey mate,' he said, 'are you a fucking Pom?'
I had never before heard the term "Pom", had no idea what it signified, and the whole delivery of the question seemed to convey both aggression and contempt. I stared hard at him to express my displeasure. The three of them swayed together for a moment, and then my interlocutor decided to repeat the question even more provocatively. Still I didn't understand, but I sensed a most unpleasant insult.

I don't know what possessed me to do it, but I got to my feet. They appeared almost too drunk to stand up, but it might have been mock drunkenness. If so I could be in real trouble. But I had to do something. I faced them down.

The whole bar went quiet. It was like the classic moment in a Western, when the saloon brawl breaks out, ending with smashed chairs and people falling through balsawood balconies. I continued to face them down. All I really wanted was for Butch Curwen to appear from nowhere and save my skin.

Then all at once, my aggressor caved in.

'Aw shit' he said, and turned away. I sat down, almost collapsing with relief. The three of them staggered out. To my astonishment a round of applause broke out, mostly from the Maoris. Suddenly I was some kind of hero. Perhaps they even thought I was one of their number. One of my friends said;

'Jeez, we thought you was going to take em.'

I shook my head wanly, and tried to pretend it was all in a day's work.

'Tell me,' I said. 'What did they mean..... what is a Pom ?'

'Oh it's just a word they use,' he said. 'It just means an Englishman. A "Pommy."'

'Oh,' I said. 'Next time I'll know.'

Chapter 23

Returning to Iwakuni we joined in the normal peace time routines of an R.A.F. base, with flights by Corsair fighters, Mustangs, and occasional transport aircraft. Our camp cinema and club, which had been justly signposted 'The Nip Inn', began to show signs of festive adornment and we became aware that Christmas was almost upon us. Most of my group were too freshly arrived to feel twinges of seasonal homesickness, so we prepared to enjoy the period as best we might. We had every confidence that the food would be exemplary, but a slight worry began to emerge about what might be available to foster liquid celebration. Throughout the year our steady tipple had been a form of light ale which came in half pint bottles and bore the discouraging label 'BEER. Allied Forces For The Use Of.' Underneath that was the admission, rather than the claim, 'Brewed by the Dai Nippon Brewery, Tokyo.' We ascribed the label to the warped sense of humour of some catering officer. It was a chemically orientated concoction, innocent of hops, which had to be tolerated rather than enjoyed.

Already we'd had one unfortunate case of a Leading Aircraftsman, normally a very pleasant fellow, who was prone to bed-wetting, whereafter he woke up, climbed into someone else's bed, and proceeded to try and repeat the performance. One night he tried to do it in Mac's bed. Mac found this quite unacceptable, threw him out angrily, and next day we felt we had to report the problem to authority. It was diagnosed as some form of 'D.T's', ascribable to the beer, and the offender was given medical attention, followed by repatriation.

Perhaps that was his whole intention, we never knew.

There followed much discussion in the hut about how we could obtain something more acceptable to drink, when the season of good cheer began in earnest. One of the older hands mentioned that there was a place up in the mountains, not too far away, where it was possible to buy the Japanese rice wine 'Saki' in any desired quantity. I had tried 'Saki' once or twice, found it much to my taste, and every bit as strong as Scotch. I asked how we could get to the place, and was told, "dead easy". All one of us had to do was apply to the Officer i/c Motor Transport for permission to borrow a jeep one week end, and we were away. Stan worked in M.T and I asked him if he could arrange it. He said there should be no problem.

A week or so later, Stan reported that all was well, and we could borrow a jeep the following Saturday. We made a little collection, and I planned to buy a couple of Magnums, which ought to see us through.

On the appointed Saturday Stan and I went to the M.T. yard and he indicated the jeep we could use.

'Looks good,' I said, 'A nice white one. You sure you can drive okay?'

'I'm getting me licence soon,' he said, 'We'll be alright.'

As soon as were on the road, I felt apprehensive. Stan could work the gears well enough but he seemed to be wrestling with the steering wheel rather more than was necessary. I felt the urge to

Kintai Bridge, Japan

say 'Let me drive mate,' but I held back. One didn't want to insult a friend. We passed through the town without incident and stopped at a tea house near the famous six hundred year old Kin Tai Bridge, which was alleged to be that shown in the Willow Pattern Plate, and used by the absconding lovers.

It was an exquisite spot, the stone bridge built in a series of hoops over a foaming river. We drank coffee and ate cakes, each one crowned with a single Heinz baked bean, a typically aesthetic Japanese offering. The Tea house was in fact run by the Australian WVS but we were served by a charming Japanese girl in traditional dress. Music was provided by a wind up gramophone which boasted only one record; Bing Crosby singing "Deep Purple." As soon as it stopped, little Lotus Blossom rushed in and dutifully wound it up again.

We resumed our mission, but a few miles on, the metalled road gave way to dirt, and I found myself becoming positively nervous as the vehicle slid around bends with precipitous drops on one side. Then we saw two R.A.F. figures, walking. We stopped and offered a lift which they were glad to accept. One of them I knew, a quietly confident Londoner called Peter Thornton.

At last we reached the house which I took to be the distillery. I went in and said, "Saki kudasai," and indicated two magnum bottles. After much bowing and smiling they were produced, money changed hands with several "Arigato Gozaimases", and I returned to the jeep, indicating that I would sit in the back, cradling them in my arms to avoid damage.

Stan started up the jeep and we began the return journey. Downhill, sliding around bends, his driving was even less competent than before.

Suddenly an old man on a bicycle appeared, and Stan swerved violently to avoid him.......

***

Trauma is a wonderful phenomenon, a blind drawn over body

and mind, obliterating pain and all the memories associated with it. I heard a voice say 'Dave's alright, he's only winded.' I protested 'I'm hurt. For Christ's sake get an ambulance.' My only further recall of the hours or even days that followed, was a brief flash of consciousness in an ambulance, and a nurse's voice asking 'Is he an R.A.F. boy?'

When I eventually began to regain full consciousness it was clear that I was in a hospital bed, heavily strapped up around the middle. There was blood transfusion gear around me, and a male nurse stuck a needle in my arm from time to time. I was coughing a lot, which caused quite a pain, and someone held a receptacle for me. There seemed no good reason for staying awake, so I dozed off for long periods, day and night. In one waking period I heard a Tannoy message calling for a 'Flight Lieutenant Broughton.' If it was he who wielded the scalpel that saved my life, I offer him belated thanks.

One morning, eight thousand miles away in Snowdon House my mother answered a knock at the front door and knew this was something unusual, because most people came to the kitchen door. The very sight of a telegram boy would have prepared her for bad news. In six years of war many mothers and widows to be had received them. They almost knew what to expect.

Her eyes would have misted over as she read it. It told her that her son was in hospital, dangerously ill at Iwakuni, Japan. There was a telephone number she should ring for further news.

She called my father in his office and he returned home at once. He telephoned the number which was that of an R.A.F. Headquarters department. He was put through to a sympathetic officer who said that he had no further news; but he went on to explain that the R.A.F.and the Red Cross had instituted a special service whereby the nearest relative of any personnel whose life was in danger overseas could now be flown out to be at the sick man's bedside. If my father wished to avail himself of the offer would he please be at such and such an R.A.F. office in London within forty eight hours to join a regular flight to the Far East.

There was not a moment's hesitation. He packed a suitcase with the necessary documents. My brother drove him to the station. There followed a nerve wracking period of delay over inoculation certificates, but his niece, now in London, provided the necessary ones and eventually he took off for Hong Kong. There he was transferred to an unheated Sunderland flying boat, so cold he could only eat his food wearing gloves.

In Iwakuni hospital, my first inkling of this extra-ordinarily decent gesture by the RAF authorities was to be told by a hospital orderly that my father was on his way. It was almost like a hallucination when two days later, I awoke from a well-doped state to see him standing at the foot of the bed. He looked quite exhausted. The Sunderland had been an uncomfortable and deafening experience, and he had a streaming cold. I managed an appropriate comment.

'My God, Dad, you look worse than I feel.'

He was given accommodation in the officers' quarters, and soon formed a good relationship with the medical officers. There is always a rapport of this kind when doctors get together no matter how different their origins and experience. Presumably they had not been told of any silly bureaucrat's ban on coloured pesonnel in Japan, and in between visits to me they gave him a jeep and driver to ferry him about.

I spent the next few days drifting in and out of consciousness thanks to regular doses of morphine. I was aware of plentiful aches and pains, and was heavily stitched up around the centre section. I became aware of a certain dependance on the opiate. The staff were all male and one felt grateful for the extra strength of male arms as they moved one gently about, doing what was necessary. The most disturbing aspect was coughing up blood which gave the Medics much concern. I was able to form a rough idea of the damage sustained; one kidney removed and other bits repaired. Broken ribs were of little consequence because I wasn't going anywhere; but the products of damaged lungs continued unabated. I received a visit from Peter Thornton, and began to realise how much I owed him. It seemed Stan had swerved on a mountain bend and gone over the edge. The other three had jumped or been thrown out. I had stayed idiotically in the back desperately hanging on to our bottles of Saki, and ended up underneath. It was Peter who got me out, sent one of the others to phone for an ambulance, and wisely prevented me from drinking water a farmer's wife had offered. Next he obtained a spade, and buried the broken glass, knowing that R.A.F. police would soon be on the scene and draw the wrong conclusion. I learned later that Thornton had been a keen Boy Scout in his youth, and I was forced to conclude that if this was what Baden Powell had been about, in forming that Empire wide movement, maybe there were one or two things I should forgive Imperialism for. Poor Stan, it appeared, had been put under arrest and was likely to be charged for failing to fill in the necessary transport application, and taking a jeep without authorisation, It just so happened that it was the Commanding Officer's personal jeep, painted white, and it was in the garage for extensive repairs to the front suspension and steering.

None of that helped poor Stan's case, and it seemed to me that all my service problems were destined to involve Commanding Officers. Nothing less would do.

Days and nights concertina'd themselves as they do in a well doped sick bay routine, but one became aware of regular uninvited visitors in the shape of cat-sized black rats that climbed in over the door. Shouts of "Rat!" came from the livelier patients, whereupon the ward orderly would rush in loosing off an air pistol in all directions. I had one memorable night when I put out my hand to reach some chocolate on my bedside cabinet, and grasped a handful of fur instead. Waking up next morning I assumed it to have been a feverish nightmare, until I saw my empty chocolate wrapper in the middle of the floor.

My father came in regularly but obviously felt too embarrassed to spend long periods at my bedside.

And then came Christmas, and with it the further embarrassment that I was to be the star of the medical show. It seemed the R.A.F. authorities had decided to use the whole business of 'Father flies to sick son's bedside' for publicity purposes. There was a Forces' newspaper, and an enthusiastic article was written showing, not without justification, what decent chaps Air Vice Marshals were. On Christmas day a jovial Aussie lady Squadron Leader/Matron arrived and poured me a glass of sherry, while cameras flashed all round.

The story was even printed in a Japanese paper, and someone sent me a 'get well' present of carved bamboo. By then, if I had felt twinges of guilt along with the internal spasms, I was now being made to feel a complete phoney. Here was I, an Aircraftsman second class, who had been involved in a somewhat dubious enterprise, being treated as though I were an air ace who had shot down thirty enemy aircraft in the thick of fighting.

But the official care and solicitude was only just beginning. The doctors were well satisfied with the results of their surgery, but they could do little about my lungs. The medical C.O. came to a decision. I needed to be sent to a proper chest unit with X rays, and skilled operational facilities. There were two alternatives, San Francisco and Sydney, Australia. There were regular flights to Australia, so there it would have to be. Someone raised the question of my father and the M.O. answered without hesitation.

'That's alright. He can go as medical escort.'

We got ready for the flight, which would take three days in a converted Lancaster. At the last minute they decided to remove the forty or so stitches around my middle before the flight, to avoid any risk of infection. I watched with some concern as they undid them, and my centre section appeared to open up as if by zip fastener. Not to worry though; they produced about thirty feet of bandaging and wrapped me up like a deceased Pharoah on his way to a newly built Pyramid.

One of the orderlies came over to ask if I needed anything before the flight. I hadn't had a shave that morning and asked if there was any chance of getting one. He nodded and went off, returning a short while later, followed by a little old Japanese man who reminded me of a Netsuke carving. He bowed low and proceeded to unroll a pack of traditional Japanese razors, slim bamboo sticks with gleaming blades attached. He arranged a sheet and deferentially began to lather my face. There followed a perfect shave without so much as a "nick", and he concluded with a smile of satisfaction When I rewarded him with a bar of chocolate, his joy knew no bounds. He packed up his things and proceed to reverse out of the room, bowing seven times as he went. My father and I exchanged glances of delight. It was a performance of pure mediaeval Japanese theatre.

My farewell to Japan had put the clock back five hundred years.

For the flight, I was strapped to a stretcher which was fastened to the floor. The C.O. flew part of the way with us, over a bumpy mountain range. He sat bracing himself against the bulkhead and instructed me to place my feet in his back so that he would become a human 'shock absorber.'

All the way South, via Manila in the Philipines and Darwin in Australia my main concern was for my father, still not recovered from his first flight, and now having to rough it for several more thousand miles. And the new Labour Government's monetary plight meant that he had been allowed to bring just £5 cash for a world-encompassing journey that would have impressed Jules Verne himself.

Chapter 24

The Concord Rehabilitation Hospital in Sydney Australia was built in the thirties specifically to care for wounded servicemen. It was ultra modern, ten storeys high, with picture windows, every known capability, lavishly equipped and staffed. When my father set eyes on it he felt he had seen a vision of the future. To anyone from Britain, a hospital was normally an inadequate, dark, mid Victorian edifice with cockroach infested kitchens and a staff struggling to pull it into the twentieth century.

I was wheeled straight into a chest ward, and at once the X rays began to roll. My father was contacted by the RAF medical adjutant, who greeted him warmly and installed him in comfortable quarters. I was put in a ward with six beds, and soon able to form a positive view of the other occupants. They were welcoming, considerate, good humoured, and very Australian. It was they who started me on a lifelong study a la Margaret Meade of the national disposition, temperament, language and origins. Most relevant was that these men had all been 'through the mill' in some way or other at the hands of the Japanese in the far East, or the Germans in the Western desert. They would have regarded the youths I had confronted in Tokyo simply as 'raw prawns'. The first man to invite me to his home was in fact a veteran of the First World War who had been gassed in the trenches, and returned every year for treatment. He had a taste for classical music, and regarded Mendelssohn as greatly underrated.

My treatment included prolonged physiotherapy sessions, with a nice nurse thumping my chest back and front with cupped hands. I seemed to make steady progress, and was even able to contemplate Australian breakfasts which inevitably included lamb chops and, to my astonishment, Guinness. The whole world knew that Guinness was good for you, but Australian hospitals accepted the proposition as gospel truth.

I settled in easily, joined in the local banter, and quite began to enjoy life. Harmless little jokes were played on the nurses like putting one entertainer's Ventriloquist's dummy into a bed, and scaring the night nurse with his near death appearance. After a few weeks I was even well enough to enjoy a little Occupational Therapy, making plates and pots in the appropriate department.

But it wasn't all fun. As a chest patient I had been warned by older hands that I was going to have to undergo an ordeal which was likely to bring out every ounce of latent cowardice that I possessed. It involved something called a 'Bronchoscope', and had been developed by a refugee surgeon from Vienna. Today it is a common enough practice but in 1947 the available technology was primitive and fearsome. Concentric tubes were pushed into the mouth and down the windpipe into the lungs to allow surgeons an internal visual examination, and at the same time extract any infected mucus. On the appointed day of torture there were at least six trainee doctors present, and since no general anaesthetic was used, it took three of them to hold me down. The tube felt about the same diameter as a scaffolding pole, and grated against the teeth, as one felt oneself choking to death and fought like a wildcat, while interested voices above one discussed the finer points of what they could see and even smell.

My slow, agonising death throe seemed to take hours, and when the show was finally over they wheeled me back to the ward, where I stayed skulking beneath the sheets in a mixture of shock and shame. Within three days however, Hippocrates had worked his miracle. The coughing had stopped. I was on the mend.

My father's expression of relief when he looked in was a sure sign that his world-encompassing journey had not been in vain. He, meanwhile had been treated like a visiting professor, shown all Concord's many facilities, and been given a tour of perhaps the most attractive city in the British Commonwealth. He must now plan his journey home for if he stayed longer, he knew that his own job might be in jeopardy.

The Air Force could not offer him a flight back to the U.K., and rather than wait many weeks for a sea passage he booked a flight, at considerable expense, on a civil airline. The day before his departure he came to say 'au revoir'. We stood at the hospital entrance and I endeavoured to express my apologetic gratitude for all the trouble I had put him to.

'I have to thank the R.A.F. medical authorities,' he said simply,'they've been absolutely marvellous. And what really matters is they've got you well again. The Adjutant here has been a great help. When I get home I shall send him a little 'thank you' present.' In due course I found out that he and my mother had bought a solid silver salver and sent it by sea mail.

In the weeks that followed I started to make genuine friends among my co-patients. They were mostly in their early thirties and one called 'Don' fitted the national ideal perfectly. He was tallish, good looking and affected the slightly bloody minded demeanour and speech that was very much favoured. It could be off-putting to a newly arrived 'Pom'; but it was he who made sure that I was on all the hospital 're-hab' outings that took place. One such was a typical coach trip to Katoomba in the Blue Mountains to enjoy fresh air and spectacular scenery. At lunch time, Don heaved a packing case out from the storage bay and broke it open to reveal a mound of lamb chops and sausages. He then built and lit a fire on some rocks and cooked and served all those on board. As always, the Guinness flowed freely.

It was my first ever experience of a 'Barbie'. Any later ones I have attended in England have been pale, windswept imitations of the real original in the Aussie 'Bush.'

On another occasion Don announced that he was off to the races at Rosehill and 'would I like to tag along?' He studied form and betted quite heavily, and I was relieved that he ended the day in credit. I confessed I knew nothing about horses, put my pittance on an outsider in each race and lost the lot. Don was not surprised. To an Aussie, gambling is pursued nation-wide with religious intensity. You don't mess around. You study it. You live it. So much so that on the day of Australia's greatest horse race, the Melbourne Cup, one of the ward sisters came round with her 'book' taking the bets of any patients who were bed-ridden. It was part of the Australian way of life; all of a piece with fillet steak for breakfast if you wanted it.

Don's own professional activity was a matter of speculation. It was said that he hired out the deck chairs on one of the beaches. He also seemed to have show-business inclinations and a day to remember came when one of the Marx Brothers visited the hospital. Don took charge of the proceedings. A small group of us gathered round the piano, the newsreel cameras whirred.

Like a practised professional Don pronounced;

'Ladies and Gentlemen, I give you, that great Hollywood star...

Mr Chico Marx!'

The celebrated clown grinned manically, looked around and asked 'Where's the wops?'

He then performed his standard piano piece using an orange to play the bass notes. It was a moment to cherish. Somehow or other I had succeeded in joining the R.A.F. and ending up appearing on film with the Marx Brothers. Perhaps Groucho would like to think about making a movie and calling it 'The Big Crash.'

But Don had one final and supreme piece of miscasting to offer me. One afternoon when I had been watching him and the others playing bowls on the hospital green he said to me,

'Coming on the big parade tomorrow Dave?' 'Parade', I asked stupidly, 'What Parade is that?'

'The Parade' he said. 'The Anzac Day Parade. The greatest day in Australian history.'

'Oh,' I said 'sorry, I didn't know.'

He shook his head sadly at my unforgivable Pommy ignorance. Meanwhile I had to think quickly to make an excuse.

'Sounds great,' I said, 'But I couldn't march. I'm not up to it.'

'You don't have to march,' he said, 'You go in a car. We lot all go in cars.'

That put the matter in a different light. This could be a good chance to see Sydney like a proper tourist.

'Oh, that's great,' I said, 'I'd love to come.'

There were a dozen or so spacious 'limos' which we wounded war heroes occupied while waiting for the bands, and the contingents to march away. I had never witnessed anything remotely like it. This was the day to celebrate Antipodean nationalism, to remind the world how they and their fathers had stepped in to save the Mother Country in her hour of need in two great wars. To the cynic it was also a reminder of Winston Churchill's disastrous plan at Gallipoli when thousands of Aussies fell victim to Turkish gunfire. To me as a naive interloper it seemed like Armistice Day, the Changing of the Guard, and a New York Ticker Tape parade rolled into one.

I sat in a back corner seat, looking at the cheering, flag wagging crowds six deep on all pavements, and painfully conscious that if any real Australian patriots had known my true status, they would have been inclined to haul me out and tar and feather me.

But there was no point in trying to hide, I was there to be seen. Suddenly, as we bowled along, I saw a very pretty girl, flag in hand on the kerb. I could not resist a second glance. She caught my eye, gave a huge affectionate smile and a furious wave of her flag. In that moment I knew why national leaders and film stars behave as they do; I had experienced the intoxication and sheer power of celebrity status, something the forthcoming age of Television would make our daily diet.

However much I might have been inclined towards guilt at my phoney situation it did not seem to bother my real ex-service Aussie friends in the least. They were all experienced enough to know that the moment a man puts on a uniform, anything might happen to him. He has no control over the dangerous situations, or the lethal hardware he finds on all sides. You do what you are ordered to as part of any daily routine in action or out of it. If there are dangerous explosions you bite on the bullet hoping one from the other side will not kill you. You try not to be a coward; but I have been told many times by people who sported medals, that when the whistles blew, they were frankly scared to death. All weapons of war are dangerous at all times when you get too close to them.

A shell may explode by accident; or your aeroplane may simply crash in fog like Squadron Leader MacIntyre's.

'Friendly Fire' is a common experience. Or your mate may simply put your jeep over the edge. All metal is hard stuff.

Meanwhile my sojourn in Concord was adding another dimension to my youthful experience which was quite unexpected, and which I came to appreciate profoundly. It was all about being among Australians.

Australians were well known to have what might charitably be called the strongest possible reservations about their British connection. They had a firm view of Britain as a class-ridden society and they held two different stereotypes of the English. One was the public school officer class who considered himself utterly superior, but in fact made a pretty poor showing when it came to truly manly things like playing Rugby, or winning Test Matches or fighting wars. The other working class stereotype (which Orwell shared) was that

'Strines

of the depressed member of the working class, who had bad teeth, rarely took a bath, and was always 'whingeing'

More literate Australians of course put aside such stereotypes; they had heard about the "Blitz" and they knew what Britain could produce in the worlds of ideas and entertainment.

My colleagues however were far from being well read. Their creative urges found outlets in everyday speech. So I had to begin to wonder why I seemed to be so well accepted by those around me. It wasn't just the fellow feeling of ex-servicemen. I might have had every reason to expect them to be antipathetic. Not only was I a 'Pom', but the 'White Australia' policy was a deep rooted thing, and I could very easily have been put on the receiving end of that.

I reached my conclusion only years later, 'recollecting in tranquillity.' I guessed that Australians liked me because they regarded me as something of an 'outsider'. I didn't fit any British stereotypes. I was expected to have attitudes pretty much like their own; developed by generations who had been literally dumped in a hostile land, told not to come back, and to make what they could of it from their own resources.

As an explanation it seemed as good as any.

Soon after Anzac Day I received a 'distinguished' visitor from home. Someone who, once a 'Pom' from Bristol, now fitted the Australian ideal to perfection.

My brother's wife had written to a relative called Herbert Harris who had emigrated to Australia after surviving the trenches in the First World War. He had built up a sheet metal business, from nothing, sold out to General Motors, acquired a 'spread' with sheep numbered in tens of thousands and lived in a fine house by the sea at Cronulla, presided over by Florence, his wife. As soon as I was fit to travel he came in his spacious Dodge and whisked me away for a few day's taste of the high life.

Millionaires were something I only knew about from left wing literature, but I found him most congenial company. He was chunky, tough, and matter of fact. His wife 'Flo' took me to the cinema (advance booking essential) and then to experience the essence of Australian living at nearby Manley beach. The surf looked irresistible, but all I could manage was a few breast strokes which the local lifeguards and muscle boys were kind enough to ignore. They decided I was neither waving nor drowning. I also yielded to a habit I have taken years to break myself of; I got on a horse. This one obviously came from the Northern Territory, and wanted to go home. I had to swear profusely at it to turn it round.

In one of our chats at his local golf club, characterised by fruit machines and young bloods plying pretty girls with pink gins, Herbert embarked on a serious chat which both flattered and disturbed me. With his entrepreneur's capacity for instant assessment he raised the question of my future after I was demobilised from the R.A.F.

'Haven't really thought, Herbert,' I told him honestly. 'Been too busy recovering, I guess.'

'Well,' he said sincerely, 'You ought to think about staying on out here. It's a great country. Look what it's done for me. You can do anything you like if you're ready to work hard. I'd help you get started.'

I realised with pride that he had taken a shine to me. He was practically offering me a job. Then he touched on a more sensitive aspect.

'You'd have no problem with immigration.' he said, 'Not sure about your father, but you'd have no problem.'

The qualification was well meant, but it brought my whole life into focus. I was tempted to say 'I wouldn't want to live in a country my father couldn't live in.' Especially after all he had just been through on my behalf. But it would have been ungenerous of me. I knew about Australian immigration rules. In time they would be modified to the country's benefit, but in 1947 the climate was hostile to say the very least.

I still had plenty of time to think, however, and meanwhile, as if the medical authorities were not being generous enough to me already, they invited me to spend a couple of weeks at a convalescent home called "Lady Gowries". This was a luxurious house in the country once owned by a Governor General's widow. Among its most memorable features were the bathrooms, one of which was finished entirely in black tiles. The forest surround gave a sense of the range of Australian wild life, and included birds that made a sound like a cracking whip, and others that sounded like a church bell.

I also met there a charming man in his late twenties whose name was Henry Brook. He told me that he had changed it from "Heinrich Bruch" and his family had escaped from Vienna at the time of Hitler's "Anschluss". Opting for life in Australia, he had undergone the full stringent Naturalisation requirements, and worked for three years in the outback, herding and sheep shearing. Meeting him gave me a sharp reminder of what the last few years in Europe had been all about.

His experience did, however, keep me thinking about Herbert's generous offer. I hadn't the remotest notion of what I wanted to do. The idea of taking some dull job appalled me. There was only one alternative though, and that was to go to University, as I knew my father dearly wished me to. At the very least that would give me a few years in which to think. Bristol University did not appeal to me. In the sixth form at B.G.S. we had felt ourselves to be somewhat superior to the undergraduates there.

The only real pull seemed to be towards Oxford, and there was one man I knew who could open that door; my ex Headmaster, John Garrett. I remembered once he had read us some letters of Rupert Brooke, as perfect examples of what letter-writing should be. I sat down and tried to write him a letter, as close as I could manage to, in the style of Rupert Brooke.

After more than a year as a fully paid up illiterate, it didn't come easy.

Chapter 25

Back among my ex-service friends I made closer acquaintance with a young man who would prove to be my greatest benefactor in 'Oz' and who set up a situation which came close to making me change my mind about going home. He was known as 'Hobbsy' due to the Australian trick of adding a letter 'y' to words to make them congenial; no one ever used his first name, and indeed I never found out what it was. Nor did I know what he was suffering from; there was a convention in the ward that one didn't ask. If a chap wanted you to know he would tell you. Hobbsy seemed to take to me immediately, perhaps because we were the two youngsters among older men. He had been in the Australian Navy, and his father was something in shipping. This meant that he had plenty of spending money, and received lavish indulgences from his dad. He was an only child and his mother was never mentioned.

Quite early on he had taken me on a shopping expedition to one of two of Sydney's lavishly stocked department stores. He was immensely keen on dress, and proudly claimed to own at least a dozen pairs of what he called repeatedly 'slacks'. He insisted on my buying a pair too; this meant that my uniform disappeared into a tin truck so that I almost forgot its existence, and seemed at times to run the risk of being classed as a deserter. Together with the slacks came a choice of smart open necked shirts, shoes and a 'cardy', which seemed standard Australian wear rather than a sports coat.

Hobbsy took me out to stop over at his Dad's place where I also made the acquaintance of the most recent gift from the doting parent, a horse; a rather fine hunter of over sixteen hands. He challenged me to ride it, and I made a brief excursion on its back which ended in my treading down some rose bushes, and almost wearing out my welcome. I was no horseman then, nor ever would be. More to my taste would be the next present Hobbsy had been promised by his father. The latest bright red M.G. TF two seater sports car which was due to arrive in the showroom very soon.

With all these indulgences showered upon him it would have

been easy to give way to envy; but I was content simply to be alive and well, and in any case Hobbsy's friendliness was so overwhelming as to neutralise any competitive instincts I might have.

There followed several more shopping trips to town with further purchases, for him at least, of differently styled 'slacks', and shoes, and for me a close up introduction to the renowned Sydney Harbour Bridge. I found myself intrigued by the lavish array of British made goods in the shops, in particular the colourful tableware and decorative pieces from Doulton; it seemed the British export trade was already well under way.

And then I got to meet Clare. One had been aware that Hobbsy was engaged, his fiancée had not been to the hospital, but she joined us on a shopping trip.

Back in the ward, Hobbsy came out with a bright and generous idea.

'Look,' he said, 'you're just hanging around here. Clare's dad owns quite a few properties around town. How would you like to move into one for a few weeks? I'm sure I could fix it.'

I said it sounded absolutely wonderful.

'Great,' he said, 'I'll have a word with him.'

A couple of weeks later I was cordially invited to a special occasion where I would meet the whole family and friends. It was Clare's twenty first birthday party, and it was held in her father's main house, a Victorian terraced property in an area appropriately called Paddington. There was a spacious parlour at the rear with a table big enough to accommodate twenty or so and a goodly spread of food and soft drinks. At the head sat a smiling Hobbsy and next to him the glowing birthday girl. She was blonde, charming, and I thought her quite beautiful. I was introduced to the parents, and her father was particularly jovial. Among the guests were two Chinese, one of whom had brought a guitar.

It became clear that there was a special kind of bond between most of those present, and later when I was able to tax Hobbsy on the subject, he gave a full explanation.

'Living Gospel Church,' he said, 'Old man Johnson's an

Evangelist.' He flies all over the place. Doesn't overdo the preaching though, they like to sing a lot. He's a pretty nice guy. He's off to Singapore next week.'

I dismissed any thought of comparison with my Uncle Sammy's church. Certainly these folk seemed determined to enjoy life, and didn't ban coffee or cinemas.

Thus the scene was set for a period of recuperation which surpassed anything I would have imagined possible, in a setting that few other countries could have provided in terms of climate, good living and pleasurable self-indulgence.

Hobbsy made good his offer of a place in town, and brought about a situation of pure, gold embossed fantasy.

'Look,' he said enthusiastically, 'The Johnson's have gone away. The best place for you is their house. There's only Clare and her granny staying there. They'll look after you.'

If 'Little Red Riding Hood' qualifies as the ultimate fairy tale, it must have a lot to do with the Wolf moving in and in this case there wasn't even the need to disguise oneself as a grandmother.

The house had a little sun loggia at the front, big enough for a single bed. There were some wicker armchairs, a table and a 'player piano' with a selection of jazz music rolls. There I was installed. Clare occupied a bedroom at the rear, and granny's room was at a midway point. It transpired that she was Polish, and hard of hearing, which I found no great disadvantage.

On my very first morning, as the Antipodean sun roused me, there was a knock on the door and a smiling, lovely, twenty one year old Clare stood there in a summery dress bearing a tray of breakfast things. Dream sequences came no more heavenly than that.

During my first few days, I was all gratitude and consideration. Clare seemed never to stop smiling, and I maintained a perpetual grin of appreciation. We talked about England, Australia, life in Sydney, Japan and Hobbsy. I expressed an interest in the Player Piano, and soon we were singing along with Bing Crosby and Hoagy Carmichael numbers. On the third day the phone rang, and Hobbsy asked to speak to me. I said how much I was enjoying myself, and he capped my pleasure with a suggestion beyond any I might have hoped for.

'Look,' he said, 'Clare likes to go out a bit, so why don't you keep her company. I wouldn't mind at all.'

It was the final green light. I could now start on an interlude that grew more pleasurable with every new sunny day that dawned.

We began the very next day. We explored, we roamed, we commuted, we ate and drank at open air cafes. We crossed the bridge, took harbour trips, cooed at the wallabies and koalas in Taronga Park zoo, cackled at the laughing jackasses in the botanical gardens and window shopped like any romantically involved couple. It was quite obvious that Clare enjoyed my company and my appetite grew by what it fed on. Naturally I had twinges of guilt, but these were totally obliterated when I had to go to Concord for some tests and spent a night back in the ward. Hobbsy was his usual chummy self, and then I caught an inkling of a fresh development that put my situation in a wholly acceptable light. There was a new night nurse on duty and it became clear that she was paying supererogatory attention to Hobbsy. After dark she was at his bedside for hours on end. Suspicions were confirmed when Don made an acid comment.

'I'm getting pissed off with this,' he told me, 'Whisper, whisper, whisper, all night long. We're all bloody fed up with it.'

So that was it. Clare's fiancee was intent on grazing new pastures. I was providing him with just the space he needed to operate in. I had no intention of sitting in judgement on his activity, least of all telling Clare about it. I merely took a good look at the nurse concerned and wondered how he could bear to waste his time with her, when he had lovely Clare waiting in the wings. So was my flat in town a whole devious plot to allow him to do his thing? I had never been taught to ascribe the most pejorative motives to human actions, and I really preferred not to go down some path that Henry James might have taken, with much verbalisation in the process. To be charitable perhaps he had just grabbed the opportunity as it arose, and when Clare was conveniently otherwise occupied.

'Charitable explanation', I thought. I'd better stick with

that' Even so he was taking a risk. Did it not occur to him that I might become a serious competitor? Was he so confident that he imagined no-one could displace him in Clare's affections? Endless speculations were possible, but there was no point. I simply went back to Clare with renewed enthusiasm reinforced by a sense of moral legitimacy.

The year of 1947 marked a post-war explosion in the world of fashion. The extravagances of Christian Dior came to affluent Australia long before they did to ration booked England. A street photographer preserved for all time my recuperating persona, walking arm in arm with a lovely girl who wore the 'New Look' months before it reached Knightsbridge. And as always the time was commemorated with its songs. We went to see a lively musical. There was a catchy number in it all about Spring and life in the country. "Out of town" was the refrain, and we sang it or hummed it day after day.

Nothing is quite so corny as the notion of "our song", but surely one does not have to make excuses for metaphorically dancing through waving wheatfields when one is in the process of reaffirming life itself, with every possible orchestral accompaniment. Those were a few weeks of fulfilled adolescent passion, which happen all too rarely. And in a world soon to be dominated by sexologists and practitioners in the technology of lovemaking, I urge anyone to rediscover the tremulous power of simply holding hands while watching an appropriate classic movie. "Brief Encounter" will do nicely. 'G'''spots are nothing compared with the intensity of passion aroused by ten fingers entwined while time stands still.

Which is in no way to decry the emancipation wrought by the great prophet of the Nottingham coalfields. We had long since learned that a hard of hearing Polish granny need present no obstacle to two young lovers. With or without daisy chains.

***

And then as quickly as it had begun, it ceased. The message came for me that an Australian Navy troopship called the 'Kanimbla' would be leaving Sydney for Southampton on such and such a date, and this much indulged Airman, second class, was required to be on it. I had just a matter of days to force myself into a decision that would probably dictate the course of the rest of my life.

One route lay towards Herbert Harris and his promise to 'see me right', perhaps in the company of a lovely girl who would herself have some problems to sort out. The other route was back to the complicated but solid home of my upbringing, where two devoted parents who had suffered somewhat, truly deserved to see me again. A world full of known intellectual stimuli that I had begun to sample but was then forced to abandon, which had bred in me a whole complex of intellectual ideas and urges, against a backcloth of worldwide political events.

"Two roads diverged..... and sorry I could not travel both."

Besides, perhaps something in me had already begun to crystallise matters when I wrote that letter to John Garrett. In just twelve months I had seen and experienced more than most people do in a lifetime. Perhaps it had to be enough.

One thing I knew I could not do was say goodbye to the others I had met and liked. I have never been good at goodbye's. Leaving parties, wakes and the like, fill me with pain, and I take the coward's way out, sneaking off in a silent shamefaced manner, unable to face people I would probably never see again. I investigated the contents of my trunk, to make sure I still had the remains of the uniform I had once worn every day.

But Clare was a special case. She took the news sadly. On my penultimate day she said;

'I'll take you and show you the oldest building in Australia.' It seemed an odd thing to suggest, but it proved remarkably appropriate. We caught the tram to a spot near the harbour and sat on a grassy bank. I was vaguely aware of a dignified looking classical building, but my thoughts were for her. Fortunately there were no tears, only smiles. Always smiles with Clare.

'Can't I come back to England with you?' she suggested, half seriously.

'Maybe I could put you in my kitbag." I said stupidly

There was little more to say. No 'come you back to Mandalay.' She looked hard at me and said, shaking her head thoughtfully,

'I don't know what it is about you. You're not handsome.'

No terms of parting endearment were expressed. Not a hug, and certainly not a kiss. It was over. Cole Porter wrote a beautiful song about such moments.

Neither of us was aware, and I did not discover until many years later, that the building we had glanced at, was the work of someone who came from the very town I was now destined to return to. He was an early convict settler, from Bristol, called Francis Greenaway, and he had built several fine buildings in Clifton, before falling foul of the City Fathers, and being sentenced to transportation.

At times Australia can seem quite close to home.

Chapter 26

The ship I was told to report to was called the Kanimbla and I was seen aboard by an army transport officer who, ignorant of my lowly RAF rank, offered me a glass of sherry, which I politely declined. He gave me the choice of joining an Australian navy mess or travelling alone in the sick bay. Having good rapport with the Aussies I chose the former and was not disappointed. They proved a most affable group, one with a slightly gay demeanour. There was also a R.N. lad returning home to Wales, and a chunky farmer's grandson from West Australia who felt obliged to point out to him that "my granpapy's farm is bigger than your whole country." The most noticeable presence however was that of a jovial six foot Greek called Papadopoulos. I was to see what a favourite he was; it augured well for the country's growing multi-racialism.

The Kanimbla was carrying several hundred men to Portsmouth to take over a British aircraft carrier which would become the 'Sydney'. Imperial ties were still strong enough for such things to happen; equally, if it was a cash transaction, the hard up mother country certainly needed the money. Although there was none of the sense of adventure experienced when outward bound, it was a pleasant voyage. We stopped off at Melbourne and Perth where Papadopoulos ran foul of the local constabulary after a boozy exploit with a fire extinguisher, and next day the entire mess marched to the Police Station to apologise on his behalf and successfully plead for his release.

After Oz we saw no more land until we reached Suez, and one gained a new sense of the ocean's vastness. Out at sea the term 'roaring forties' was heard. Furious winds raged for several days and it was noticeable that the Ship's Tannoy System stopped broadcasting the previous day's mileage, suggesting that we had been simply wallowing around without progress. This had a secondary advantage for those from the U.K. because Test match scores were also being broadcast, and England were once again failing to win back the 'Ashes'.

I may be able to lay claim however to inventing a new shipboard sport. I found a tennis ball in my locker and began bouncing it off floor and locker and catching it repeatedly. Rapidly this developed into a competition and complete obsession. People were coming 'off watch' asking "what's the score?", and after a quick shower followed by liberal Johnson's baby powder, resuming the contest until it reached astronomical figures. I believe 'locker tennis' has since become an obsession with most of the world's navies, but I am bound to feel that I could not have been its sole inventor. Probably a Russian did it first.

The entry into Gibraltar had momentous overtones. Here at last was the very essence of the British Empire, the towering rock of British Power, the clenched fist flourished by Britain at the rest of the world, shaken over the centuries at the Spanish, the French, the Germans, the very keystone of Britain's world-spanning arc of naval power, defiant and untouched by rulers from the Sun King to Bonaparte, Hitler and Stalin.

As we slid into anchor, we saw a living symbol of all that power, a renowned British cruiser, bristling with armaments. There was just one difference. This famous cruiser, once called the Achilles, and berthed ahead of us was no less than the victor of the battle of the River Plate. And it was now the refurbished flagship of the Indian Navy, re-named the 'New Delhi.'

The handing over of a British warship to the newly re-born country of the great pacifist Mahatma Gandhi could hardly have been anticipated by my father and his Labour friends at their crucial Party Conference in 1944.

In the town itself, the sudden arrival of 2,000 sailors from such disparate parts of the old Empire must have given the authorities some concern, since the High Street was no bigger than that of an English market town, and with all those servicemen white and brown, milling about sampling British beers in Spanish bars, 'incidents' might well have been expected. The Army police were much in evidence and two enormous Redcaps paraded magisterially up and down.

But in truth there was no cause for concern. The Aussies were on their best behaviour and the Indians felt no urge to riot, now that they controlled their own destinies, and had their own battleship. I found myself drinking equally with my own mess mates and Gurkhas who had once been in the 4th Indian Division.

Three days later, as we docked at Portsmouth, I felt an odd sense of anti-climax. There were no cheering crowds on the quayside, simply my father and mother looking strangely isolated and out of place, waiting to drive me home.

***

Returning after a long, incident-filled absence requires an unexpected psychological adjustment. All the drama is inside one's head, not in the place one has returned to. Because the individual feels strange, he expects people and places to respond as though in the third act of a classical drama. But in fact life has continued pretty much in the same way as it did when he left.

Jobs and houses are run just as they did before. If the returning prodigal expected a dramatic response to his or her return there will be disappointment and, in the case of true returning warriors that can even produce resentment and aggression. In my case, I soon realised that it fell to me to conform, to pick up the strings and adapt to what the Americans used to call 'normalcy.'

My brother's wife baked a cake and offered a 'welcome home' party. When I telephoned Austin I had to explain my identity, my acquired Australian accent being unrecognised. Most other old friends were doing their own things. The occurrence of his own twenty first birthday party helped acclimatisation and my own followed soon after.

He was due to go up to Oxford in October, and other friends had been busy pursuing their own careers, so it soon became clear that I would have to be motivated. The years of school leaving idleness and self-indulgence were gone for good.

To that end I made an early call to John Garrett to whom I had written from Australia.

'David,' he said warmly, 'come and see me as soon as you can.'

I called at school a few days after and he gave me a sympathetic greeting. 'I really don't know what you've been doing' he said, 'Jumping into volcanoes or something equally undesirable?'

He invited me to walk with him to a bookshop in Park Street.

'It's a new one called the Pied Piper,' he said. 'Very nice, they don't mind you browsing.'

Before we left he chose a book and handed it to me. It was a newly published long poem by Vita Sackville West called 'The Land'

'You need something pastoral,' he said thoughtfully, to help you recover.' In the fly-leaf he wrote

'David Datta dedit J.G'

As we walked back to school he raised the question of Oxford.

'I've written to Bowra about you,' he said. 'There's a place for you at Wadham. You'll be getting a letter from the Dean, John Bamborough. He may invite you to take the entrance exam. Whether you do or not is entirely up to you. Either way, the place is yours.

I saw Garrett several times in the months that followed. Once was an invitation to come in for lunch with Glynne Wickham who had just been given the chair of drama at Bristol University.

'Brilliant OUDS Producer at Oxford,' he explained. 'He'll become a great name in the theatre.'

The lunch was decidedly awkward. I was well out of my depth and had little to say to a rising luminary of the stage. Fortunately the school head-boy and others kept talk bubbling along. In future years I came to hear much talk of Wickham and I kept an eye on his career. He wrote many learned tomes on the history of the theatre, and attended many conferences at Universities all over the world.

He also helped Sam Wanamaker design the Globe. But it seemed to me that the West End theatre and Broadway managed very well without any contribution from him. The Old Vic Theatre School produced far more famous actors than the University, and the one B.G.S. boy who became a big name in drama, Peter Nichols, didn't even go to University.

Such contrasts sowed in me a seed of cynicism about academics, and what they do or don't do that has grown quite rampant over the years.

I was invited by Garrett to join him with two friends at a Bristol Old Vic Theatre production of a new play called 'Wilderness of Monkeys'. This was set in a public school and dealt with boys, masters and wives. I found it entertaining without becoming a second "Mr. Chips". In the inevitable bar-room analysis after the final curtain I found myself holding forth to one of Garret's friends about the possibility of a homosexual interpretation of the plot. He listened keenly to my words of wisdom without making a comment. It seemed I was blundering into territory where my own naivete was positively overwhelming.

On another occasion, I joined J.G. as I had started to call him, on a motor trip to pick up some rocks for the school garden. The car was driven by an ex head boy whom I knew to be a brilliant scholar and athlete called David Skinner.

I could hardly have forseen the future significance of the occasion and again my naivete was quite laughable. David Skinner became a clever journalist with Cassandra on the Daily Mirror, then took Holy Orders at Cambridge, and became a minor celebrity in the Church of England. He was utterly devoted to Garrett and on his retirement they settled together in a house near mine in Wimbledon. I glance at future years only to underline my own simple mindedness about such relationships. In those days the term 'gay' simply meant 'pleasure seeking.'

To me, if two chaps lived together it simply meant that they got on well together, and shared interests. I had a lot to learn about W.H.Auden and his friends. I sensed too that my father was a little wary of my being drawn into Garrett's more adult circle. He needn't have worried; my pursuit of femininity continued at a normal pace. But I did feel that J.G. liked me a great deal. I behaved always with as much wit and affability, as I could muster, and it must have been to this that he responded. As I understand it there are certain physical types of male to which such people are normally drawn. Being dark, and somewhat saturnine I didn't see myself as in any way the type conforming to sculptures by Michelangelo or Donatello. Dad had no cause for concern.

While waiting for my entrance exam paper to materialise I set about pursuing a self-imposed syllabus in English literature to make up for a lost year on airfields and ships. I gave Wordsworth a thorough going over and even read mammoth works like the 'Prelude'. I formed a preference for Coleridge which would go down well among the literati. I even dared to flip the pages of 'Paradise Regained', which only proved the greatness of 'Paradise Lost'. My normal study routine was to get on my motor bike and take books out into the country. It was a most enjoyable period.

Eventually the exam paper arrived and I dealt with it quite confidently. In due course I received a letter from Bamborough telling me I had passed, and would be most welcome at Wadham College.

CHAPTER 27

Ours was the first generation to discover the lure of France after the war. Over Christmas Austin mooted the proposal to try and hitch hike to the Cote d'Or, and I agreed to keep him company. It proved harder than anticipated. Traffic was light and there were almost no motorised holidaymakers. Two male hikers did not appeal to French drivers in quite the same way as a heterosexual pair might have done. However we drank our fill of the real France in the way that modern airborne travellers never can. Cezanne's Mont St. Victoire remains long in the memory when you trudge the whole length of the dusty, cicada- shrill road that passed it. We spent a scary night at Avignon in a semi derelict castle run by a hunchback.

We stayed under canvas at a 'camp volant' near Cannes and drank in the atmosphere that had brought thousands of well-heeled Brits to settle there. An unexpected point of interest was a huge American aircraft carrier, anchored about a mile off shore. This was identified as the U.S.S. Coral Sea, 'the biggest goddam aircraft carrier in the world.'

It seemed I could never escape my childish interest in warships, and after a few days Austin announced that he proposed to try and swim out to it.

'I'm pretty sure I could make it,' he said, 'But if you're not up to it I'd better go alone.' I considered matters. I had borne up pretty well for a semi-convalescent, and the water was warm and inviting. 'I'll tag along,' I said, 'If I feel it's getting too much I'll turn back.' Austin was a far better swimmer than I but on the due day, the Mediterranean felt wonderfully buoyant and calm, and one could tread water for hours if necessary.

The leviathan grew more and more immense as we approached it, and after half an hour or so we found ourselves gazing up at the massive walls of an iron fortress.

'Well done,' said Austin. I felt fine, but had no idea what we might do next, as we floated around and caught our breath. Then we noticed a human being. High up and leaning over the rail was an American crew man, starring at us with no small suspicion. Austin sought to avoid any confrontation. He waved an arm in greeting and shouted;

'Hi! We're British!'

The Yank continued to gaze down intently, his gum-filled jaw moving steadily. He gave no answering greeting.

'It seems we're not welcome,' I muttered to Austin. We turned and began to head back to land. The moment encapsulated Anglo-British military relationships. Successive British Prime ministers would learn painfully that the Americans love to have us 'on board' provided we did as we were told and didn't get in the way of the guys with the real fire power.

On our swim back Austin once again led the way with his powerful crawl. I made several stops to recover and when I did he moved even further ahead. It was then that I saw a possible drama start to unfold. We were far enough out at sea for Cannes and other coastal towns to be mere lines of distant white buildings. It suddenly dawned on me that Austin was mistakenly heading, not for Cannes but some other coastal town. It looked as thought it might be Frejus, and if so it was many miles further away. Even a water polo "Blue" like Austin might well fail to make it.

I shouted at him, but he was too far away to hear. I shouted again but to no effect. Then I made a quick decision. I set out to swim for Cannes as fast I possibly could. After many panting minutes I came to the beach where a flotilla of 'Pedallos' lay beached. I seized one of them, climbed on, and began furiously pedalling towards the diminishing figure of Austin.

By now almost exhausted myself, I at last caught up with him. He looked pretty short of breath himself.

'Good God,' he gasped,'where did you spring from?'

'Grab hold of this,' I said and without further talk began making back for Cannes. It was enough for me to see that he really needed the tow. When we made it to the beach, he smiled a little wanly.

It was enough to tell me that I had done the sensible thing. The incident was closed but afterwards, I had to reflect on how little thought my companion had given to my situation, plodding along behind him, and concerned for his welfare.

Returning from Cannes we discovered that we might well make Paris in time for the Bastille day celebrations, which ought not to be missed. But a hard coming we had of it. No-one seemed inclined to give us a lift and after three days we were in a state of some exhaustion. Such that we booked into a Paris hostel on the afternoon of Juillet Quatorze and made straight for our beds. We woke up in the small hours of the following morning and must have been the only two people in Paris to have missed the whole thing. All I saw was one tipsy piano accordianist playing to an audience that had long since dispersed.

We did not dare leave Paris without some taste of culture, and found it determinedly at the Paris Opera. There was a performance of Bizet's 'Pearl Fishers' which created in me a lifelong affection for the music, though sadly not an overwhelming dedication to the art form that my father and many of my acquaintances have felt. I still cannot respond well when a twenty stone tenor kneels down to kiss the hand of a 6 ft three mezzo soprano and sing "e gelida manina." The "honte" I confess, is entirely "a moi."

I was also pleased to attend one of the first great post-war art exhibitions, that of Gaugin at the Orangerie. Austin did not join me. By then a certain incipient coolness had developed as it often does after such expeditions, and he headed back across the channel. I felt good at seeing the Gaugin but in all honesty never felt the same regard for his technique as I did for his lamented onetime afficionado in the Yellow House.

That summer ended for me in Ilfracombe. If culturally anti-climactic I nevertheless felt I had a duty to devote some time to my parents who had booked a holiday in a hotel there. I was invited to play at the local tennis club and there met a very attractive girl whom

I drove home and took sherry with. She had a fiancee who was up at Oxford and confided that he had problems with the course he was reading, which included Philosophy. The profoundly questioning discipline did not mix well with his religious convictions. In the event I myself took the same degree and had no such problems. My own problems would stem from a lack of critical tuition which did nothing to assist my comprehension of the subject.

My father had by then settled down to a life of reduced political activity and approaching retirement. He continued to lecture to St. John's Ambulance Trainees and he kept alive the Bristol Indian Association which he himself had founded. One of his greatest pleasures was found in ballroom dancing, which he and my mother pursued avidly, even winning certificates of merit. My mother particularly valued the opportunity to put on 'glad rags' and spend pleasurable evenings with the man she had married nearly forty years before and so often lost to the demands of politics.

To confirm their newly discovered suburban activities my father one day made a dramatic little gesture.

'Nana,' he said one day. 'I never bought you an engagement ring. To celebrate our many happy years together I would now like to do so.'

He drove her to the best Jewellers in Whiteladies Road, Mr. Punchard's and there she was thrilled to be encouraged to choose a diamond ring. Having done so my father then made a gesture which typified his approach to such matters.

'Thirty years is a long time to be happily married,' he said, 'I think the occasion demands a second one. Against all her cautious Gloucestershire instincts my mother was seduced into buying a second ring. 'To keep the first one company.'

But even more dramatic plans were taking root. It was clear to us that when he reached retirement age we would have to leave the house I had been born in. They would have to find some little place to retire to.

A Golden Wedding party

'Without all that housework, thank goodness,' was my mother's view. Len Robson's father, a man of property, helped them look for one; and old friend Stan Burgess warned him against areas which were scheduled for planning development by their own Labour council. My father's salary had always been about as low as any doctor's stipend could be. But we had lived all those years in Snowdon House rent free, and thanks to my mother's cautious budgetary control, their financial situation appeared to be viable.

Indeed, my father's natural optimism led him to make a 'promise' that would incur truly lavish expenditure. Once settled in the new house, he would show his loyal wife ('My Rock of Gibraltar,' was his favourite tag) the country of his birth. Not just a fleeting visit, but a prolonged journey during which he too would discover the place he had helped to set free; from the Punjab in the North, to Kerala in the South, from Bombay in the West to Madras in the East.

Not once in all those years had he been able to make such a journey; his politics, his profession and his family had made it quite impossible. And there was one spot in particular that he dearly longed to visit, the place of his own birth in East Bengal.

For there in a village, soon to be made part of a new country known as Pakistan, lived a frail but still bright eyed old man, ready to confront any who might come and try to evict him from his home.

It was his brother Ullaskar, now famous as a revolutionary hero, and the man who had been responsible for his coming to England in the first place.

EPILOGUE

When my father had left Concord Hospital the RAAF had kindly driven him to Mascot Air terminal He boarded his plane with plenty of time to spare, and chose a window seat. The plane soon filled up, but there remained a vacant place next to him. A few minutes before take off a flustered late-arrival came aboard and made towards it. My father looked up and saw a face that seemed to strike a faint chord in his memory.

'Is this seat taken?' asked the passenger.
'No, it's free,' said my father.
The latecomer stowed his hand luggage and collapsed breathlessly into the seat.
'Only just made it,' he panted.
'Did you have traffic problems?' father asked.
The man glanced at him and gave a toothy smile.
'Nay,' he said, 'my problem's autograph hunters. They won't let you alone.'

The smile had done it; "teeth like a row of gravestones," someone had once said. The autographs confirmed it. Father experienced a brief re-wind of memory. He was back in Bristol Grammar School with my old headmaster, posing the problem of a son, utterly devoted to a North Country clown who sang risque songs and played some sort of ukelele.

He regained his composure. After a few moments when he had settled in he asked,

'Is it possible you are Mr. George Formby?'
'The very same,' said George.

'Oh, I'm delighted to meet you,' dissimulated my father. 'My son is a great admirer of yours.'
'Glad to hear it,' said George with a grin.

My father began to steel himself at the prospect of a whole day and night in the company of the entertainer who had caused him so much concern a few years earlier. They settled down while engines roared, and flight staff went through their paces. Conversation was not to be expected while they underwent the familiar drama of take off.

Soon the expected meal was served, and the usual comments were made.

Although my father loved conversation, the company of a celebrity was a most inhibiting situation. Soon he thought it best to introduce himself formally.

'My name is Doctor Datta,' he explained.
'A doctor eh,' said George. 'Always good to have a doctor in the house.'

My father went on to explain his odd journey. George said he had done a lot of entertaining of the troops. "Even had lunch with General Montgomery," he said proudly.

Any long haul flight is characterised by long periods of dozing, a modicum of reading, and sporadic bursts of conversation.. The hours passed awkwardly. At one point father recalled the film of George's that I his son had once dragged him resentfully to see.

'It was about the Air Force,' he said. George became quite animated.
'"It's In The Air,"' he said proudly. 'We had a lot of fun making that. Beryl said it was the best thing I ever did.'
'Is Beryl Mrs. Formby?' asked my father perceptively.
'Best wife a man could have,' said George, 'My business manager too. I'd be nothing without her.'

They went on to agree about the importance of a good marriage.

Hours passed. Below then Africa slowly slipped by. At one point my father asked George about the instrument he played.

'It's a Banjulele,' George explained. 'A cross between a banjo and a Ukelele. I started playing it when I was a kid. Bought my first one for two quid. The fans love it. Funny thing is I can't even read music,' he admitted. My father was moved to mention his own adolescent ambition to sing opera. It created a certain bond between them. George was impressed that my father could sing and speak Italian. The subject of success and failure came up again.

'I never expected to be world famous,' said George. 'It just sort of happened. They kept on wanting me to make more films. They were sent all over the world. Even to Russia.'

'To Russia?' asked my father, genuinely astonished.
'Aye, it seems Uncle Joe loved them. He insisted we send them during the War. On the Arctic convoys'
'I never knew that,' admitted my father.
'And do you know something else?' pursued George, 'they gave me a special prize. An Order of someone or other.'
'An Order?' queried my father.
'Aye, Order of Lenin,' said George. 'That's it, The Order of Lenin.'

'Good God,' said my father.

The sheer improbability of the notion reduced him to silence. But George was warming up.

'Tell you something else, Doc.' he said. 'They say I'm the only Englishman ever to be awarded it. Think of that. Lovely thing it is.

Beryl keeps it at home in the side-board.'

Many tiring hours later, the plane began a gentle descent. They roused themselves in anticipation of a landing. George had made the flight before, and he had something special to impart.

'Tell you what, Doc,' he said, 'We're just coming into Algiers. Now, back home you can't get eggs for love nor money. Still one a month on the ration. But I know a place here where you can buy plenty. If you like I'll take you there. Your wife would really appreciate it.'

My father agreed. They took a taxi to the Casbah and each bought a box containing thirty eggs. They nursed them on their knees all the way back to London.

On arrival at London airport my father followed the star at a respectful distance. A crowd of fans waved and cheered as George Formby, Order of the British Empire, and Order of Lenin, stepped towards the throng, smiling broadly, but with both hands clasping his precious purchases.

Few of the onlookers paid any attention to my father, but any who did probably assumed that George had acquired an Indian servant somewhere on his travels, who was carrying an extra box of eggs for him. My father collected his luggage and caught the coach back to Bristol.

***

A FAREWELL TO EMPIRE

DAVID DATTA

ACKNOWLEDGEMENTS

This book contains no more fiction than the average biography. I would like to thank all those people mentioned whose solicitors will not be in touch with me, and in addition Frank Cioffi, Martin Datta, Anne Bradley, Raymond Smith, Rohit Barot, Paul Vaughan, Rozina Visram and the executors of David Garnett. I am also indebted to the internet, to the authors of the 1944 Labour Party Conference Report, and above all to my wife Margaret who nobly suffered my many months of pure self indulgence.